THE DIVINE PASSION

ROBERT G.
HAMERTON-
KELLY

THE DIVINE PASSION

REFLECTIONS ON THE PROPHETS

The Upper Room
Nashville, Tennessee

THE DIVINE PASSION

The scripture quotations not otherwise identified are from *The New English Bible*, © The Delegates of the Oxford University Press and the Syndics of the Cambridge University Press 1961 and 1970 and are reprinted by permission.

The scripture quotations designated RSV are from the Revised Standard Version of the Bible, copyrighted 1946, 1952, and © 1971 by the Division of Christian Education, National Council of the Churches of Christ in the United States of America, and are used by permission.

Excerpts from *The Jerusalem Bible* are copyright © 1966 by Darton Longman & Todd, Ltd., and Doubleday & Company, Inc. and are used by permission.

The scripture quotations designated KJV are from the King James Version of the Bible.

The scripture quotations designated AP are the author's paraphrase.

Book Cover: David Weilmuenster
First Printing: March 1988 (5)
Library of Congress Catalog Card Number: 87-051429
ISBN: 0-8358-0580-8

Printed in the United States of America

To Grace Mortsolf
who quietly makes a difference

CONTENTS

THE DIVINE PASSION

INTRODUCTION

*O Jerusalem, Jerusalem, killing the prophets and stoning those who
are sent to you! How often would I have gathered your children
together as a hen gathers her brood under her wings, and you would
not!*

—*Luke 13:34,* RSV

The great Jewish interpreter of the prophets, Abraham
Joshua Heschel (1962), described their experience of God as
sharing in the divine pathos. The prophets experienced God
as one who longs for a relationship of love with all his
creation and especially with his human creatures. For the
prophets, God is not aloof and remote; rather he goes in
search of his beloved creatures; he yearns for them; and
because he is God the creator, the creatures sooner or later
have to deal with him. If they will not have him as friend and
lover, they must have him as judge.

Samuel Terrien (1978) goes even farther than Heschel in
the interpretation of the divine pathos. Because of the element
of judgment in God's dealings with us, he often has to act in
ways that cause him pain and shame. "He suffers as he
convicts. He wounds himself as he destroys" (265). For
instance, when in the eleventh century B.C. the ark was
captured by the Philistines (1 Samuel 4:11), it was a humiliation for God that he willingly bore because he could not allow
unrighteousness to pass unpunished. A prophetic poet dis-

11

cerned in that incident the evidence of God's judgment (Psalm 78:59-61). God's absence from Israel's history at the time of that catastrophe was really his presence as judge. "Presence in judgement meant absence in history, but the divine decision meant a divine humiliation." Terrien suggests that we call the theology of the prophets "the Divine self-abasement," or "a theology of self-immolation." For Christians, the cross of Christ is the nadir of this divine self-abasement, and that is why the prophets are so important to an understanding of the gospel.

We are the heirs of the prophets not only because the Old Testament is part of our scripture but also because our Lord Jesus Christ is the culmination of this prophetic experience of God's yearning for us. In him, God who had spoken in times past through the prophets spoke to us in his own person through his only son. Like the vineyard owner whose messengers had been mistreated by the wicked tenants in the parable (Mark 12:1-11), God ultimately sent his son, believing and hoping that the tenants would honor him and give him his due. He was disappointed, for they not merely cast out the son as they had cast out the servants he had sent, they also killed him, believing that by so doing they would gain possession of the vineyard. "O Jerusalem, Jerusalem, killing the prophets and stoning those who are sent to you!"

This allegory of the history of God's relationship with his people presents the matter of our hostility to God in commercial terms; we prefer to own rather than to rent our lives, and we are even willing to steal and to kill in order to win that independence. We withhold from God the acknowledgment of his ownership of our lives by refusing to receive his messengers or to pay the rent and by killing his son and heir. The rent is not only a symbol of God's ownership but also a means by which we stay in touch with him. By stealing the vineyard, the tenants say that they do not want the ongoing relationship with the owner that regular payments of rent would mean.

The allegory also presents Jesus at the end of the series of messengers whom God has sent and whom we have rebuffed, the son whom God hoped we would honor. Jesus is the last and the greatest of the prophets, the culmination of God's communication with his creatures, a prophet and more than a prophet as a son is more than a messenger.

The Old Testament prophets are, therefore, an essential part of the spiritual heritage of Jesus, and the light that the major themes of their message cast upon the gospel portrait of Jesus enables us to see many features of that portrait that we might otherwise miss; no theme is more illuminating than the theme of the divine pathos, the passion of God.

Heschel has written that "all of human history as seen by the Bible is the history of *God in search of Man*" (438). God is in search of man because he cares about us enough to miss us. After hearing a sermon on the prophet Hosea, someone came up to me and said, "Now I understand why it is important to be regular in prayer; because God misses me when I am not." The astonishing notion that God can miss me, like a parent misses a child away at college or a lover misses the absent beloved, is perhaps new to many of us who are accustomed to think of God as absolutely self-sufficient, needing nothing and no one. Whether we find it new or even strange, it is this understanding of God that the biblical prophets had and that Jesus not only shared but expressed at an unparalleled level of intensity in his death and resurrection as we Christians understand them—namely, as his suffering of our hostility against God and his overcoming it without revenge or retaliation.

Heschel calls this quality of God "the divine pathos"; we prefer to call it "the divine passion," chiefly because *pathos* is not a common word in the average vocabulary and secondarily because *passion* has that double reference to the desire of God on the one hand and the suffering of Christ on the other. We wish to link these two themes very closely, and *passion* achieves that linkage in a word. God passionately desires a relationship with us and is prepared to suffer the rejection (undergo the passion) that we in our sinfulness inflict on him as he seeks to enter into a relationship with us.

CHAPTER ONE

COMPASSION FOR HUMANITY,
SYMPATHY FOR GOD

The prophetic message is central to our faith not only because of its content but also because of its source. The source of the prophetic word is God himself; the prophet speaks the word of God. Through the prophetic consciousness, certain crucial things that we could not have found out for ourselves have been revealed to us. This understanding is why the scripture says that even Jesus our Lord, who is more than a prophet to us, is at least also a prophet. He stands in the tradition of those who reveal God's nature and God's will to us—they by speaking God's word, he by incarnating it in his living and dying in addition to speaking it in his teaching. Our basic definition of a prophet, then, is one who reveals God. In addition, however, the prophet is also a poet, a preacher, a patriot, a diplomat, a social critic, and a moralist; he is all these things, but fundamentally the prophet is the spokesperson for God.

The prophet's human words, spoken in the ordinary situations of our lives—our personal life, our business life, and our political life—reveal the will and the nature of God. God is intimately involved in all of life. Nothing is too trivial for God to care about. God's presence is not only in religious places and experiences but in the secular events of life as well. Our business, our politics, and our personal lives are the arenas of God's activity, and it is there that we obey or disobey him.

God is involved in all of human life in a human way and

through human means. Not through thunder and lightning; not through voices from heaven, miracles that override our centers of judgment and strike us dumb; but through the human words of our fellow human beings, God makes himself and his will known to us. God gives himself to us in the human experience of a herdsman like Amos, an aristocratic statesman like Isaiah, a young maverick priest like Jeremiah. Notice that among those three only one is professionally religious—Jeremiah. In those days in order to be a priest, all one had to do was be born into a priestly family; priesthood was not so much a profession as a destiny. These prophets are not professional holy persons. God gives himself to us in the human experience of people who willingly take upon themselves the burden and the joy of speaking for God in their times and places.

Each one of us, therefore, can be a prophet. As God reveals himself to us in the joys and struggles of our lives, so can we bear witness in word and deed to that revelation. God in his providence has chosen to use human channels. Your words and mine can become the word of God to the world if we are willing to listen and then to speak out, to speak out of that deep place in each of us where our lives touch God's life. It is from that place in each of us that moral and spiritual energy comes; it is from that place that the light streams that enlightens every person who comes into the world. The prophets are not essentially different from you or from me. They too speak from the deep place where their lives meet God's.

If we have not yet discovered that place in our beings, the words of the biblical prophets can lead us to it as they tell us of the nature of God and his presence in the world. What the prophets tell us is well summarized in the phrase used by Heschel, "Compassion for humanity, Sympathy for God."

The prophet expresses God's view of the world. He experiences God's presence so vividly that he sees with God's eyes and feels with God's heart. The prophet represents God's compassion for humanity, and that is why he agonizes over the plight of little people. When one reads Amos, Hosea, or Isaiah, one cannot help comparing them with the Greek Homeric epics, for Homer is an exact contemporary of these prophets. In the *Odyssey*, for instance, the only little people who appear are Eurycleia the nurse and Eumaeos the swineherd. They are both slaves and in the story are merely adjuncts to the heroes. The ethic of Homer is heroic and aristocratic; the little people are like cattle, merely fodder for the heroes' wars and schemes. Justice is entirely a matter for the aristocracy, a balance in the dealings of the powerful. The weak have no claim on justice; they are at the disposal of the strong.

In contrast, Amos, Hosea, and Isaiah, exact contemporaries of Homer, cry out for the ordinary folk who are cheated and exploited by the great and sent to die in the wars of the heroes. It is absolutely remarkable to observe this difference in moral sensibility. The democratic passion of the prophets is unparalleled in their time and is still pertinent today. It is behind the great movements for equality and justice in the modern world. Marxism itself has been called a secularized version of prophetism, and Marx in his better moments was clearly not unmoved by his Jewish heritage, even though he sought to repudiate it. Wherever the little people cry out for justice, wherever they fight for freedom and dignity and assume that God has given them a right to be dignified and free—wherever that happens, God is acting in passionate love for his human creatures, and prophecy is taking place, for the prophet is consumed with God's compassion for humanity, which is called justice.

The other side of the prophetic experience is sympathy for God. The prophet is not the champion of an abstract ideal; rather as representative of the living God who cares, the prophet understands the hurt and disappointment that God feels when his children reject him and act self-destructively.

Perhaps parents who have suffered the agony of a wayward, self-destructive, alienated child can understand this best. The prophet, with a heightened sensitivity to God, participates in the divine agony; where God is rejected the prophet is rejected, and he feels in his human loneliness something of the desolation of God—always on the margin, never in the text, even though he wrote the text. The prophet feels God's loss of his children, the estrangement that God's loving heart yearns to overcome. Sympathy for God.

So the prophet reveals the vibrant personhood of God. God is no abstract principle. God is not detached and aloof. Amazingly, God is humble and loving and easily wounded. God is vulnerable to his human children, tortured by their cruelty to one another, and crucified by their callousness. Compassion for humanity, sympathy for God—this is the essence of the prophetic consciousness. The prophet is the revealer of the heart and mind of God, and he stands at the center of our claim to have received a disclosure of the nature of God and God's purpose for our lives.

Prophets are frequently unappreciated because they seem so negative, and the Old Testament prophets are good examples of this. They are easily shrugged off as "fire and brimstone preachers," something commonly known to be out of date. "Tell us something encouraging and uplifting," we say, "and stop harping on our sins and injustices." But this negative aspect of prophecy is crucial to our spiritual health. It guards against that most dangerous spiritual disease, self-righteousness. The most frequent accusation hurled against today's church is hypocrisy. To that accusation, thank God, we can answer that the bulk of our sacred scripture is made up not of self-congratulation but of self-accusation for not living up to our creed; the prophetic complaint is always directed first to God's own people and only then to the nations. The prophetic complaint is always directed first to us, and in that regard it is a sign of God's love for us. It is a sign of how passionately God cares about the health of our souls, for injustice and ambition and selfishness destroy our own souls first and only then do they do damage in the world. So the prophetic "fire and brimstone" is an expression of God's care for us, a form of his compassion for humanity, an aspect of his justice.

In common language, *prophet* usually means someone who knows what's going to happen and who foretells the future. Prophets occur in religions other than the religion of Israel, and their function in those religions is indeed chiefly to foretell the future. In Greek religion the best-known prophet is Apollo's oracle at Delphi. In the Greek tragedy *Oedipus Rex* we see the awful outworking of the oracle's prophecy, and we see the prophet Tiresias interpreting the oracle. Essentially the oracle has foretold the future and the free human will struggles vainly against the message of the god.

The earliest traces of prophecy in the Old Testament are similar to the Delphic oracle. For instance, in the first book of Samuel we are told that Saul, out looking for lost livestock, goes to consult Samuel about where to look. Samuel the prophet is a seer. The great prophets whose writings are preserved in the canon are not like this, however. They forecast the future only in a general sense. There is an old Chinese saying that, paradoxically, expresses the exact nuance of this mature prophecy. "Prophecy is difficult, especially about the future." This proverb intends to say that in fact foretelling the future is impossible, but let us be literal minded. A great deal of prophecy is not about the future but is about the present, about our situation here and now, and about God's compassion and God's suffering. Some prophecy is about the future, but only about the future as it arises out of the present in roughly the following way: "If you persist in your present injustice, you will eventually, in the future, destroy your soul; and if society persists in its present injustice and oppression, it will eventually, in the future, destroy itself." Is this foretelling the future? Well, yes, but certainly not in the sense that oracles and fortune-tellers do. It rather assumes the moral truth about God and about the universe and draws a reasonable conclusion from that premise. If God is just, the doers of injustice live contrary to God; and if you live contrary to God and the basic impulse of creation, you will reap not freedom but bondage, not joy but sorrow, not life but death.

This prophetic prediction, in a general sense, is borne out in the history of nations. Nations subsist on the justice they create, and they are destroyed by arrogance and injustice. Look around you at the least stable of countries and see the truth of this. It is of more than passing interest to note that the church is the oldest continuous institution in recorded human history. Some have argued that its persistence is due to the justice and love it practices; even in its moral poverty and hypocrisy it gives more than other institutions can muster.

We might also gain some encouragement by reflecting that the United States of America is the oldest republic in recorded history after only two hundred years. (The Roman Republic lasted longer but most of that time it was not truly a republic.) I like to think that the prominence of the Old Testament prophetic tradition in our cultural heritage has something to do with the longevity of our freedoms, such as they are. Perhaps our willingness to listen, to be corrected, to change; perhaps our creed with its aspiration of "liberty and justice for all" has something to do with the longevity of our political institutions. If so, then let us be careful to continue to listen and to care for the little people who are the objects of God's compassion and whose suffering causes him such pain.

It is an astonishing notion that our injustice can cause God pain; nevertheless the prophets reveal quite insistently that it does. For God is filled with compassion for his creatures, and the prophet is filled with sympathy for God.

CHAPTER TWO

THE SOUND OF SILENCE: ELIJAH

And after the fire, the sound of utmost silence.
—1 Kings 19:12

The translation of our text that I am using is given by Samuel Terrien in his book *The Elusive Presence* (232), and much of this chapter is suggested by that book. The phrase that Terrien translates as "the sound of utmost silence" is better known by its translation in the King James and Revised Standard Versions, the "still small voice." *The New English Bible* has "a low murmuring sound," and *The Jerusalem Bible* has "the sound of a gentle breeze." Clearly the translators are at a loss to make sense of this enigmatic phrase, which in direct translation from the Hebrew says, "The voice of a crushed silence." That may not make sense to a translator, but it certainly makes sense to a poet and a prophet and anyone who has lived and struggled with God.

The story of Elijah on Mount Horeb is an opportunity to reflect on how we know God, how we experience God, and how we understand God to act in our lives and in our world. How do you identify God's action in your life? By the miraculous, wonderful things that happen—coincidences and things like that? Or by the convictions and intuitions that come in prayer and contemplation?

To be sure, there are probably as many meanings to the word *God* as there are people who use it, and even within the

Bible the meaning of the term changes as the writers come to understand more fully the nature of God and his presence in the world. The story of Elijah on Mount Horeb is a story of change in the understanding of God, and as we consider it we might ask ourselves whether we, too, like the writers of the Bible, might not need to change our understanding of God and of how he acts.

The traditional understanding of God up to the time of Elijah included the notion that God made himself known in storms, earthquakes, and fires, the impressive manifestations of nature, or in the unusual and uncanny. Whatever caused terror and awe; whatever could not be explained or contained; these things told of God. So the term *fear of the Lord,* which was used in those times as the equivalent of what we mean by the term *religion,* had a healthy component of plain terror in it. People remembered the burning bush where God spoke to Moses; the fiery, storm-shrouded mountain where God had given Moses the law; the rollback of the Red Sea where Pharaoh's army was drowned. They identified the action of God with the miraculous and the catastrophic.

Our story has Elijah on the very mountain where the law was given to Moses, the foundational event in the biblical tradition. Elijah experiences a rerun, as it were, of all the special effects of that momentous occasion. After each one of the special effects, after the storm, after the earthquake, after the fire, we are told that God is not there. We hear a threefold proclamation of the divine absence, as if someone were deliberately taking up the earlier story of Moses on the mountain and correcting it. All who thought that God was in the special effects are wrong, we are being told. We hear a threefold proclamation of the absence of God that ends in the sound of "utmost silence," "the sound of a crushed silence"— the oppressive silence of the absence of God. How many of us have not experienced this after our usual means of commun-

22

ion with God seem to have failed and our prayers seem to fall back to earth unheeded?

Elijah had come to the mountain after the well-known contest with the priests of Baal on Mount Carmel (1 Kings 18:20-40). We recall how he had challenged them to a contest. The god who could cause fire to fall from heaven and consume the sacrifice would be considered the true God. Four-hundred-fifty priests of Baal prayed all day, gashing themselves with swords and pleading with all their might to no avail while Elijah mocked them. When his turn came, Elijah was able to call down fire at a word, fire that consumed not only the flesh that had been drenched in water but also the rocks and soil of the altar. Then the people present cried out, "Elijah's god is the true God and we will worship him." A most satisfactory outcome, one would say!

But the next time we see Elijah in the story, he is fleeing for his life from the queen; he is in despair about the futility of all that his life has stood for; and he is back at the place where his religion began, the sacred Mount Horeb (also called Sinai). The victory over the priests of Baal had turned into a defeat; he had won the battle and lost the war. The people who took God's side after that display of power had been even more impressed by the power of the king and queen and had changed sides again. (It is always thus with this kind of power—external and oppressive; the effect is superficial and easily changed). Elijah's whole understanding of who he was, who God is, and how God acts had been thrown in doubt. "'It is enough,' he said; 'now, Lord, take my life, for I am no better than my fathers before me'" (19:4). He is at the point of suicide.

At this point, God brings Elijah back to the place where it all began, in storm and earthquake and fire, and tells him that he had misunderstood the nature of God's action. The final denial, that God was not in the fire, alludes to the fire that fell on the sacrifice on Mount Carmel as well as to the fire that attended the lawgiving. The victory over the priests of Baal was hollow. Even there, in his moment of greatest triumph, with the dramatic descent of fire from heaven, Elijah was out of touch with God; God was not in the fire.

There follows the sound of a crushed silence, what used to be translated as "a still small voice," as if the point of the story were that we should seek God in quiet contemplation rather than in wonders and prodigies (which is indeed part of the point, but not all). The crushed silence is what we would expect after we have been told that some of the central things we believed about God were mistaken, that ideas and experiences we had based our lives on were wrong, and that that "old-time religion" misrepresented God, even when it was powerful enough to work miracles.

In that crushed silence, Elijah covered his head and face with his cloak, went and stood in the mouth of the cave, and heard the true God speak. In the silence left behind by departing illusions, there in the emptiness of a life that had been stripped of this world's securities, coming out of the cave like a newborn from the womb, Elijah heard the true God speak.

He was told to do three things, each of which was fairly ordinary compared to his former activity. No more miracles, no fire from heaven, no running at the head of the king's chariot; just anoint Hazael to be king of Aram, Jehu to be king of Israel, and Elisha to be his own successor as prophet (1 Kings 19:15-18). To be sure, Aram was the enemy of Israel, so in endorsing their king, Elijah was making a political statement to the effect that God is with all nations and not just with Israel. In anointing Jehu to be king of Israel while Ahab was still on the throne, he became party to a projected coup d'etat. So the things God told Elijah to do were no less spectacular in their own way than calling down fire from heaven, but God had changed Elijah's arena of activity from religious show business to politics; Elijah may have been the first preacher to go into politics, but he was certainly not the last. After the silence, he was told to express his service of God and to look for God's action in the arena of human relations and political interaction. From nature to history and from the marvelous to the ordinary—the locus of God's revelation had shifted.

There is so much in this story that we could dwell on to our great profit. Let me mention just a few points among the many that have no doubt already been seen simply in the telling of the story.

Firstly, there is the religious virtuoso reduced to the point of suicide when all that he believed and based his life on lost its meaning and fell silent, yet he is given a new understanding and a new mandate after the silence. Some of us have known that experience of loss and have tried to deal with it by returning to the old religion we remember from the time when faith was alive and exciting to us. A short time ago someone I had not seen in ten years came to tell me that he had recently accepted the fact that he was gay and that he had at the same time given up the Christian faith. I remembered him as an ardent evangelical Christian with whom I had had many debates. That form of Christianity had failed him. Even though it produced wonders and other satisfactions for him, it never touched his real need. We sat in crushed silence together. There can be no going back for him religiously; whatever God has for him lies ahead, and I think he shows great courage and honesty in giving up those attitudes that have not helped him and moving on to something new, even though the new is not yet in view. The sound we hear in the silence is the sound of God drawing near to us again and preparing to make himself known to us in a new way that will be adequate to our present needs.

I am greatly encouraged by this story from the Bible; it tells us that the struggles of faith are part of the living of faith; it tells us that not even great servants of God like the mighty Elijah are exempt from the struggle, the despair, and the need to grow by dying and rising again. This means that each one of us can be honest about our doubts and accept them as part of the process of growing in the faith. We can even arrive at the place of crushed silence, which is also the place of the sound of silence. In those paradoxes, we hear the gospel word that when we are weak then are we strong. When we must give up believing in things that formed our lives to this point and enter the silence, even there there is a sound—the sound of God as he draws near again—and after the silence, there is the voice of the true God setting us the tasks he has for us to perform.

There is, therefore, in this story the teaching that all of us will have to struggle with the difficulties of believing (not even the prophets are exempt from the struggle), and so we should be gentle with ourselves and with one another in these matters.

There is in this story, secondly, the change in the ways God interacts with us, from miracles and public displays of power to the inner conviction of the human heart and mind and the interaction among people in human relationships. The Elijah story stands at the point of the Bible's transition to the prophetic tradition. The Old Testament prophets hear God speaking in the depths of their own souls, not in earthquakes, storms, and fires. Their visions are subjective, their experience ordinary. Terms like "God speaks" are metaphors; the prophets do not hear literal voices; rather the conviction of God's will for them and their time arises in their subjectivity, and then they speak out or act; their human words become the word of God for that occasion. This new prophetic understanding of God enables Israel's religion to survive the destruction of the state and its religious institutions; borne in the heart and mind and human community, religion essentially is becoming independent of place or political power.

The prophets are able to hear God speaking in the ordinary things of life and to see God acting in the actions and interactions of human beings. God works his will through those who will let him, those who will be obedient to him. They put their own lives at God's disposal, and they call upon others to do the same. Their passion for justice and their call for repentance is an expression of the conviction that unless we do God's will, God's will will not be done. Justice depends on the willing hands and hearts of people who want to cooperate with God in his work in the world.

God tells Elijah that there are seven thousand in Israel who have neither been unfaithful to him nor bowed the knee to Baal. These are the remnant through whom God wills to do his saving work, those willing to let God work through them. It is the faithful church, the community that is open to God's guiding and that is willing to reach out to do God's work in the world. We should understand our churches today in this way, as parts of the remnant, the community of those who are willingly open to hear God speak in our midst and in our individual hearts and are willing to do what God wants us to do. In this way we would be a truly prophetic community, a truly biblical people.

Thus, the Elijah story tells us that painful moments of despair and loneliness can be the necessary prelude to a new understanding and a new and deeper relationship with God; that we must grow in our understanding of God, a growth involving painful change, even in the convictions we considered most firmly based. This story reassures us by showing how such change takes place even within the Bible itself and how even the great servants of God have to go through it. Finally, it provides us with a viable model of God's activity through the lives and work of ordinary people, like you and me, who are prepared to allow ourselves to be used by God, rather than God's activity through spectacular miracles. The story, then, makes it urgent that we put ourselves at God's disposal to do his will where we live and work.

The sound of silence which Elijah heard after the threefold proclamation of the divine absence was the sound of God drawing near to speak a new and more powerful word in his life, to reorient his ministry, and to open up a whole new way of acting in the world. When we arrive at the moment of crushed silence, then is the time to listen for the sound of the true God drawing near and to prepare ourselves to hear his word of instruction; then is the time to cover our heads in humility, to come forth from the cave in newness of life, and to hear the new word of the living God, who opens up the future for us and sets us new tasks to perform.

CHAPTER THREE

THE DIVINE JUSTICE: AMOS

Spare me the sound of your songs; I cannot endure the music of your lutes. Let justice roll on like a river and righteousness like an ever-flowing stream.

—*Amos 5:23-24*

Amos is the first of the great prophets who came upon the scene in Israel in the eighth century before Christ. He displays for the first time in Israel the deep inwardness of the experience of God which was characteristic of these prophets. "The lion has roared; who is not terrified? The Lord God has spoken; who will not prophesy?" (3:8).

In these words, Amos expresses the experience of inner compulsion that sets him apart from the professional seers, soothsayers, and ecstatics that constituted the recognized class of the prophets in earlier times. His experience of God is irresistible and terrifying, like hearing a lion's roar nearby. He does not take up prophecy because he thinks it is a good profession; neither is he born into it, like most of the class of professional seers. He is a layman and is essentially unwilling to make a spectacle of himself by speaking for God. But God is frightful like a lion as he takes hold of Amos's heart and mind, and Amos has to prophesy, no matter how reticent he might feel. There is compulsion in this relationship with God. "'I am no prophet,' Amos replied to Amaziah, 'nor am I a prophet's son; I am a herdsman and a dresser of sycomorefigs. But the Lord took me as I followed the flock and said to me, "Go and prophesy to my people Israel"'" (7:14-15). Terrien translates as follows: "Yahweh kidnapped me from behind my flock." Terrien then comments "as if he (Amos) had in mind the memory of some lamb seized by a mountain lion" (236-7).

Amos tells all the world the intimate things he experienced with God, the five visions that God showed him, and his own response to them. The visions are recorded in chapters 7-9 and are probably seen during the period from spring to fall of the year 751 B.C. The first vision, of the locusts (7:1-3), causes Amos to intercede for Israel: "What will Jacob be after this? He is so small" (vs. 3). As a result of Amos's intercession the Lord relents; the prayer of a man moves God to pathos. The same sequence occurs during the second vision, of the great abyss (7:4-6); but after that the prophet no longer intercedes for Israel, in the visions of the plumb line (7:7-9), the basket of summer fruit (8:1-2), and the striking of the altar (9:1-6). He no longer intercedes but rather acquiesces in the destruction of his people because he has come to see things from the point of view of the divine justice, the divine compassion for humanity.

It is surprising that God should destroy the people out of compassion for humanity, but what he destroys is not the good but the false, the unrepentant doers of injustice who use the festivals to appear righteous. The festivals and songs that God hates are those that give the impression that here is a people that cares about the same things that God cares about, is compassionate like God is compassionate, while the truth is that the festivals are not a celebration of justice but a phony substitute for it. Let the festivities end, but "let justice roll on like a river, and righteousness like an ever-flowing stream."

This theme came to mind some time ago as I witnessed the ceremonies accompanying the rededication of the Statue of Liberty in the New York harbor. How much of such celebration is a cover-up for injustice and unrealized ideals, and how much of it is a legitimate celebration and anticipation of a better future? After all, one of the chief ways we humans are motivated is by imagining a goal as already realized. In the celebration of liberty, as if we all had achieved it, as if there were not millions of our fellow citizens who do not enjoy the most elemental freedoms from hunger, disease, and political oppression, we could be said to be imagining the ideal in order to motivate ourselves to achieve it. We prefer to think that that is what is going on in a festival like that one in New York harbor. Nevertheless, we must heed Amos's warning and make sure that our festival serves not as a substitute for just action, but rather as a motivation to "let justice roll on like a river and righteousness like an ever-flowing stream."

We are always in danger of substituting words for action, and religious people especially are in danger of thinking that the good feelings that we get when we are together in worship, prayer, or discussion are sufficient for dealing with a problem. We should not, on the one hand, underestimate the importance of what Amos would call our "festivals," but we should be careful always to follow through in action on the things that come to us in our prayers.

The final vision of Amos (9:1-4) takes place at the autumn festival, and he sees God standing on the altar in the temple and hears God command him to strike the altar with a sword. The point is that the people's worship had become all festival and no action. The poor were not being taken care of, and even the festivals were being compromised by this lack of ethical concern and action. "Listen to this, you who grind the destitute and plunder the humble, you who say, 'When will the new moon be over so that we may sell corn? When will the sabbath be past so that we may open our wheat again, giving short measure in the bushel and taking overweight in the silver, tilting the scales fraudulently, and selling the dust of the wheat; that we may buy the poor for silver and the destitute for a pair of shoes?'" (8:4-6). While the people are present in the temple, they are thinking not about God and his command to deal compassionately, but about how to gain a business advantage, fretting about all the time they are wasting in worship.

One of the most frequent accusations leveled against church people by those outside the church is that we are hypocrites and do not practice what we preach and profess. This hypocrisy is what Amos finds so intolerable. It brings God into disrepute and makes it difficult for people to believe in him. This is why God will destroy even his own people, even at the cost of great pain to himself, because he loves all the human race and wants to reach out to those outside the church. If the hypocrisy of the church makes that reaching out impossible, the church must be disciplined by God's judgment and parts of it even destroyed for the sake of the gospel.

The most striking thing about the prophetic experience of God is that it is, at the same time, the most inward and personal and the most public and practical. Experience of God in prayer and worship and vision is expressed in public as a concern that business be honest and that the weak be protected, helped, and not taken advantage of. The church has a mixed record in this matter. We tend to emphasize one aspect of the faith at the expense of another. Either we are "spiritual" and emphasize personal commitment to Christ along with all the good things that go with it—prayer, spiritual renewal, and a personal sense of God's presence in our lives—or we are "social activist" and tend to play down the spiritual side of the Christian life in favor of participation in community action for the betterment of life in this world. Amos, like all the great prophets, was able to keep both aspects of the faith vital in his life. His spiritual life nurtured his social concern, and his social concern guided his spiritual life. After all, the God whom he served was passionately concerned about people, so how could his servant be otherwise?

Those who are rightly concerned about the need for spiritual renewal in the church sometimes give the impression that it will only occur if we return to our evangelical roots and put the offer of a personal relationship with Christ at the center of our mission and message. This is certainly the power center of the faith and should never be absent from our life as a church, but there are grave issues facing the human race that need the compassion and clear thinking of Christians in the public arena, where we deal with all people of good will for the betterment of the world.

The leaders of a number of denominations and churches have pointed us to the issue of nuclear war as the overriding public problem of our time. Amos said that God would destroy his people if they did not live their creed in the world. Now we are in a position to understand how such a destruction might indeed take place. If we do not find new resources of compassion and mutual trust, we run the risk of destroying the whole of human civilization. In nuclear weapons we see the great negativity that all our tradition has sought to warn us against—all our greed and injustice, our mistrust and envy, our violence and impatience—focused and poised to destroy us. The message of Amos has never made more sense than it does today. The bishops of the United Methodist Church, for instance, in the timely pastoral letter, *In Defense of Creation: The Nuclear Crisis and a Just Peace*, published in April 1986, have called for "a new covenant of peacemaking . . . [and] for earnest and steadfast study of the issues of justice and peace," in which we will to do all we can to realize peace with justice in the world. They say that their appeal is prophetic: "It is prophetic in that this document is our response to the Word of God. It faithfully states our understanding of that Word to our world at this moment in history."

So the prophetic spirit is still alive in Christianity; the word of God still sounds, calling us to respond to the challenges of our time, which are greater than they were even in the time of Amos. Then human injustice threatened only the nation; now it threatens the creation, and the word of God as it comes through church leaders is calling us to a "Defense of Creation." Just as Amos was seized by God from following his flock and compelled to prophesy, so we are being compelled to speak and act for God in our time. He was a layperson, and he was rather reluctant to become involved with spiritual matters, but the pressure of God upon his heart and the challenge of his time compelled and empowered him to become a prophet. There is a sense in which all of us can and must become prophets; we must respond to the pressure of the word of God upon us and offer ourselves for God's service in the public affairs of our time, as well as in the personal spiritual dimension of the Christian life.

CHAPTER FOUR

THE DIVINE PATHOS: HOSEA

O Ephraim, how shall I deal with you? How shall I deal with you,
Judah? Your loyalty to me is like the morning mist, like dew that
vanishes early. Therefore have I lashed you through the prophets and
torn you to shreds with my words; loyalty is my desire, not sacrifice,
not whole offerings but the knowledge of God.

—*Hosea 6:4-6*

We are considering the prophets under the banner "Compassion for Humanity, Sympathy for God." If the prophet Amos, with his special zeal for justice, represents compassion for oppressed humanity, the prophet Hosea, to whom we now turn, represents sympathy for God. Indeed, the phrase, "the knowledge of God," with which the quote at the head of this chapter ends, might be translated as "sympathy for God," or in more modern jargon, "empathy with God." While Amos says, "I will not accept your sacrifices—but let justice roll down like waters and righteousness like a mighty river," (Amos 5:21-24, AP), Hosea says, "I desire loyalty, not sacrifice. I desire empathy with God, not whole burnt offerings" (6:4-6, AP).

Hosea and Amos are contemporaries. They both live during the reigns of Uzziah (783-742 B.C.) in the southern kingdom, and Jeroboam II (786-746 B.C.) in the north; that is, they live in the first half of the eighth century B.C., a period of great prosperity, followed in the northern kingdom by chaos and collapse. Hosea, living in the north, experiences

35

both the prosperity and the collapse. Paradoxically, we know very little about Hosea's external circumstances, and we know a great deal about his private life. We do not know what he does for a living, but we do know that his wife, Gomer, is unfaithful and that his first son's name is Jezreel, which is equivalent in that time to "Watergate" or "Hiroshima" or "My Lai" in ours; we know that his daughter is called "Not Loved," and that his youngest son is called "Not Mine"; we know that he suffers cruelly because of his wife's unfaithfulness. Not a happy family. Mother always out with her boyfriends—and imagine how the kid named "Not Loved" must feel—only slightly worse than the one named "Not Mine" (which is probably the case biologically, as far as Hosea knew). And as for poor Jezreel—imagine applying for a job in Washington if your name is Watergate Jones or a job in the Pentagon if your name is My Lai. Not a happy family situation. A whore and three victims presided over by a whimperer.

Under Israelite law and custom, Hosea should throw Gomer out, and if she were caught in the act she should be killed, but he cannot do that. He loves her too much. "Plead my cause with your mother; is she not my wife and I her husband? Plead with her to forswear those wanton looks, to banish the lovers from her bosom. Or I will strip her and expose her naked as the day she was born" (2:2-3). Who is speaking here? Is this Hosea to his three kids, Jezreel, Not Loved, and Not Mine? Or is it God to Israel? It's hard to tell initially. But as the passage goes on, it becomes clear who is speaking: it is God. It is hard to tell who is speaking because the prophet identifies his anguish with the anguish of God. Hosea knows the pain of an unfaithful spouse, the hurt of betrayal, the loss suffered by children who are the hapless victims of such a situation. He believes that God suffers the same agony: 'O Ephraim, . . . Judah . . . Your loyalty to me is like the morning mist, like dew that vanishes early' (6:4).

The word *loyalty* used here denotes the faithfulness that makes a marriage. In the larger religious context, it describes the attitude that is appropriate to the covenant relationship between God and his people. It is a favorite word in the Psalms, where the King James Version translates it "lovingkindness." "Withhold not thou thy tender mercies from me, O Lord: let thy lovingkindness and thy truth continually preserve me," says Psalm 40:11. *The New English Bible* translates the word in the Psalms passage as "unfailing love," expressed as the love that suffers the wounds of unfaithfulness and rejection and does not fail. Unfailing love that itself bears the pain and keeps open and vulnerable and does not defend itself by repudiating the beloved and shutting down. You can see the irony then of the complaint: "O Ephraim, O Judah, your unfailing love to me is like the morning mist, like dew that vanishes early."

"O Ephraim, O Judah, O Gomer my wife, I desire unfailing love, not the sham of appearances; a shared empathy, knowledge of God not superficial, and perfunctory attention." *Knowledge* is another favorite word of Hosea's. In Hebrew, to know someone means, in the appropriate context, to have sexual intercourse with him or her. Heschel, who says we should translate "the knowledge of God" as "sympathy for God," writes as follows:

> According to the analogy of sexual union to which this verb points, this sympathy must be understood to imply an emotional experience that is reciprocal. Just as in sexual reciprocal emotion, where the feeling of one person is in no sense an object to the other, where rather both persons share the same feeling, the structure of the sympathy implied in Hosea's hypothesis is not compassion for another, but a suffering together, the act of sharing an inner experience (59).

This means for Hosea "a sensitivity for what concerns Him, a concern for the divine person, not only for the divine will, a concern that involves inwardness as well as action" (60). Amazing that one should share an inner experience with God, that one should be concerned not only for the divine will but for the divine person! Amos cares about God's will; Hosea cares about God. He shares an inner experience with God. That we should share the passion of God as lovers share, "where the feeling of one person is in no sense an object to the other"; what astonishing boldness!

Need I translate the poetry of this prophetic revelation into prose? I hope not. Old lovers know what Hosea is talking about; young lovers, too, if they are lucky. And families know the anguish and the unfailing love, loyalty, and sympathy. But did you know that our God is a lover like us, or rather, that we are lovers like God? And that our agonies are counterparts of his agony? As the first letter of John says, "Love is from God. Everyone who loves is a child of God and knows God, but the unloving know nothing of God. For God is love" (4:7-8). What astonishing intimacy! We expect God to have an imperious will that we mere creatures must obey for our own good. We even expect him to love us and care for us as some powerful parent cares for a child, and that image is present in Hosea, too. But that God should want to share love with us as humans share love—as human lovers share—that God can be pleased by our acceptance and hurt by our rejection of him—this we would not know if Hosea had not revealed it to us. The divine pathos, the passion of God. How marvelous! How human! Here is a prophecy of the great passion of God on Calvary, a revelation of the suffering love that is God's redeeming presence to a rejecting people; like the agony of a faithful spouse who shows unfailing love to an unfaithful partner.

Interspersed with these startling revelations of the divine-human mutuality are outbursts of divine anger: "I will strip her and expose her naked as the day she was born; I will make her bare as the wilderness, parched as the desert, and leave her to die of thirst" (2:3). "I will be like a panther to them, I will prowl like a leopard by the wayside; I will meet them like a she-bear robbed of her cubs and tear their ribs apart, like a lioness I will devour them on the spot, I will rip them up like a wild beast" (13:7-8). Commentators remark on the surprising nature of this juxtaposition of tenderness and fury, but lovers understand it well, do we not? It is no surprise. "How can I give you up, Ephraim? . . . My heart is changed within me. . . . I will not let loose my fury, . . . for I am God and not a man, the Holy One in your midst" (11:8-9).

What distinguishes God from mere humans is not the power to thunder or coerce, but the power to overcome fury by unfailing love. But he, this God, is human enough to know, too, those moments of furious anger at the pain. "Because I am God I will not let loose my fury." We are mortal and our emotional resources have their limits. We cannot suffer forever; sooner or later we have to shut down our vulnerability or we shall die. But God does not die, so the divine love never shuts down, never fails. The omnipotence of God is the invincible patience of the divine love. Long after we have given up loving, God loves on, suffering, seeking, succoring, sharing in an ecstasy of common emotion, shared emotion, where neither we nor God is an object to the other. There is only the deep mutuality of knowing each other in love, the Lamb crucified from the foundation of the world, the church as the bride of Christ. One flesh with God.

Hosea has the temerity to interpret his own marital unhappiness as revelatory of God's inner life. He takes seriously the claim that we are created in the image of God, that our experiences and our feelings can be a reliable guide to the nature of God's inner life. He is probably aided in this by the fact that the religion of Canaan, still alive in Israel, calls their divinity "husband and lord" (that's what the term *Baal* means) and practices sacred prostitution as one of the rituals in their cult. In this context, Hosea's message is a claim that Yahweh, not Baal, is Israel's true husband and that stable marital sex rather than the one-night stands at the Canaanite shrines is the human counterpart of the relation between God and his people. Intimate and exclusive.

For the overwhelming truth Hosea tells us is that God is a lover like us, only more passionate, more present, more persistent; a lover whose love never fails, whose love abides, greater even than faith and hope. Love will never come to an end. Are there prophecies? They will cease. Is there knowledge? It will vanish away. Are there tongues of ecstasy? They will be stilled. But love never comes to an end (1 Cor. 13). That is the message of the prophet Hosea, understood by the apostle Paul, revealed in all its clarity on the cross of Christ.

I am aware of a certain lack of equity in the imagery as I expound Hosea. The woman is the guilty one; shameful sex is a woman's crime. This feeds the stereotype of woman's sensuality as subversive of good male order and decency, and we all know that this is not entirely true. We all know that there is male subterfuge as well, but in Hosea's time the law allowed only women to be guilty of adultery; the double standard was in force. In our time we know there are quite as many faithful wives who exercise unfailing covenant love for wanton husbands as unfaithful ones like Gomer. Let that at least be said to balance the record.

Let us hear how God intends to bring Israel, his unfaithful wife, back to him. He will not threaten, he will not coerce or manipulate. He has his rage under control. What will he do? "I will woo her, I will go with her into the wilderness and comfort her: there I will restore her vineyards, turning the Vale of Trouble into the Gate of Hope, and there she will answer as in her youth"—he thinks back to the time when they were courting. "On that day she shall call me 'My husband' and shall no more call me 'My Baal'" (2:14-16).

What that means is this: "She will call me my lover and no longer my Lord (for *Baal* means the lord who owns her). No longer will she call me the Lord who owns me, but rather my lover." "And I will wipe from her lips the very names of the Baalim [as if he would kiss them away]. . . . I will betroth you to myself for ever, betroth you in lawful wedlock with unfailing devotion and love; I will betroth you to myself to have and to hold, and you shall know the Lord. At that time I will give answer . . . for Jezreel. . . . And I will show love to [Not Loved] and say to [Not Mine], 'You are my people,' and he will say, 'Thou art my God'" (2:17, 19-21, 23).

God is wooing each one of us; God invites us into a deeper and deeper relationship of love and ecstasy with himself. "I will betroth you to myself to have and to hold, and you shall know the Lord" (2:20). "And I will say, 'You are mine,' and you will say, 'And you are mine'" (2:23, AP). May it be so.

CHAPTER FIVE

THE DIVINE POWER: ISAIAH

Therefore the Lord waits to be gracious to you; therefore he exalts himself to show mercy to you. For the Lord is a God of justice; blessed are all those who wait for him.

—*Isaiah 30:18, RSV*

In the previous chapter, we considered how Hosea interpreted his unhappy family situation as a revelation of God's love for his human creatures and as a plea for sympathy with God in the suffering of unrequited love. Before that, we saw Amos interpret his experience as a man from the country viewing the corruption of the city to reveal God's passion for just dealing, especially by the rich with the poor, God's compassion for humanity. Isaiah of Jerusalem, to whom we now turn, draws on his experience as a courtier and a counselor to kings.

The horizon of Isaiah's world is international politics. If Hosea's message dealt with the pathos of God and Amos's with the righteousness of God, Isaiah's deals with the power of God; and so we are on much rockier terrain than in previous chapters. It is relatively easy to understand a broken heart and deeply moving to realize that God, too, is wounded by our infidelity and carelessness; the exposition moves on the smooth ground of inner feeling and individual experience. But when the matter is politics, consensus goes and controversy takes its place. One moves on the rocky slopes of group experience, traditional feelings. One is in the place of power.

Now the note of the divine pathos is not absent from Isaiah, as the song of the vineyard shows (5:1-7). The owner is genuinely sad that all his careful work, digging the soil, clearing the stones, planting the vines, building a tower, hewing out a wine vat—all of this has gone for naught. But notice, the Lord is an owner whose property fails to produce, not a cuckolded husband whose wife breaks his heart, and even though the prophet calls it "the vineyard of his beloved," this beloved is somewhat aloof. This beloved is the Holy One of Israel. This is the one who "exalts himself to show mercy to you."

By now it is clear that every Old Testament prophet does not say everything that needs to be said about the nature of God. Each has his own special revelation to share, given him through his own particular experience. To Hosea, Israel is God's spouse; to Isaiah, God's vineyard. To quote Abraham Heschel: "Isaiah is animated by a sense of dread and the awareness of the transcendent mystery and exclusiveness of God, and only secondarily by a sense of intimacy, sympathy, and involvement in the divine situation" (83). Isaiah loves God, yet his feeling of love occurs within the context of a wider and more intense sense of reverence and awe. This is the Holy One, high and lifted up, whose retinue fills the temple; this is the king, the Lord of the hosts of heaven, whose glory fills all creation (6:1-13); this is the disposer of nations, he who sits in the heavens and laughs at the pretensions of the powerful of this world, as Psalm 2 has it. This same Holy One expresses his sadness in the first chapter: "Sons have I reared and brought up, but they have rebelled against me. The ox knows its owner, the ass its master's crib; but Israel does not know, my people does not understand" (vv. 2-3). When God expresses sadness such as this, we are awed by the thought of who it is that loves us so.

Isaiah experiences God in his personal life. He, like Hosea, gives his children symbolic names; he lays that burden on his

44

family. And Isaiah experiences God in the domestic life of Judah. He, too, like Amos, cries for justice in town and country, but his special revelation comes from his experience as advisor to two kings on matters of international politics. He advises Ahaz (735-715 B.C.) to stay away from treaties with Assyria, and he advises Hezekiah (715-687 B.C.) to stay away from treaties with Egypt. Judah is at this time a small power caught between two superpowers. His advice is non-alignment. We know about non-alignment today. Judah, he argues, has a prior commitment, a covenant with the Holy Creator of all the nations. Trust God rather than the king of Assyria or the Pharaoh of Egypt, "For thus said the Lord God, the Holy One of Israel, 'In returning and rest you shall be saved; in quietness and in trust shall be your strength.' And you would not, but you said 'No! We will speed upon horses,' therefore you shall speed away; and, 'We will ride upon swift steeds,' therefore your pursuers shall be swift" (30:15-16, RSV). "Behold, I am laying in Zion for a foundation a stone, a tested stone, a precious cornerstone of a sure foundation: 'He who believes will not be in haste' " (28:16, RSV). But the kings of Judah were in haste, and Ahaz sped to Assyria to conclude what the prophet called a "covenant with death." Hezekiah in turn sped to Egypt to conclude a treaty that ultimately led to him being shut up like a bird in a cage, as Sennacherib, the king of Assyria, boasted after he had taken forty-six of Hezekiah's fortified towns and left him cut off in Jerusalem.

How do these passages from Isaiah apply to our present-day international politics? Is there anything we can learn from them for the conduct of international relations? Does God act in the history of the nations? Many people simply do not believe in God—the USSR officially and many of us unofficially. Some of us believe in God as far as our individual lives are concerned but not in the life of the nations; and among those believers, many find it impossible to see God's guiding activity even in the life of the individual, much less in the life of the nations. History, some believe, is a dark place of ruthlessness and power, where nice guys finish last. Then there are those, the most dangerous of all in my opinion, who believe that God indeed acts in history, always on our side to vindicate us, and that all our enemies therefore are agents of the devil to be mercilessly destroyed. And so here we sit on the verge of the valley of Armageddon; I have heard retired military men of high rank say that they believe there will be a nuclear war, that we are in fact preparing for one, and that a practiced military eye can see that our military establishment is moving in that direction. So, where is God? What does faith do now?

Let us return to Isaiah. His advice is not taken. He loses. Indeed, he was called to lose, paradoxically. Listen to his vision: "Go and say to this people: 'Hear and hear, but do not understand; see and see but do not perceive.' Make the heart of this people fat, and their ears heavy, and shut their eyes; lest they see with their eyes, and hear with their ears, and understand with their hearts, and turn and be healed.' Then I said, 'How long, O Lord?' And he said: 'Until cities lie waste without inhabitant, and houses without men, and the land is utterly desolate' " (6:9-11, RSV). Isaiah loses, faith loses. Or do they?

The prophet sees the vision of a small remnant of the people returning to rebuild Zion. He names his second son "Shear-jashub," which means, "a remnant shall return." In the midst of all the busy negotiations, the flying back and forth from treaty to treaty, the frantic buildup of armaments, God lays a precious cornerstone, a remnant whose motto is, "He who has faith will not be in haste," a remnant that trusts in the Holy One who rules the nations, and waits for him and his justice, a remnant that practices mercy and lovingkindness, of whom it is written, "We have a strong city; he sets up salvation as walls and bulwarks. Open the gates, that the righteous . . . may enter in. Thou dost keep him in perfect peace, whose mind is stayed on thee, because he trusts in thee. Trust in the Lord for ever, for the Lord God is an everlasting rock" (26:1-4, RSV)—amidst all the hurry, the speeding back and forth, God lays in Zion a precious cornerstone; God formed a remnant community of faith.

Who shall be the members of that remnant in our terrible and unprecedented times? Who shall be that remnant, if not you and me and all people of faith? More than ever, now is the time to hear and obey Isaiah's word, "Trust in the Lord for ever, for the Lord God is an everlasting rock." Standing on that rock, we shall find words to speak for God's peace and God's justice. Standing on that rock, we shall find patience, self-control, humility, restraint, and hope. We must con- secrate ourselves, each one of us as an individual and to- gether as a community, to God and God's peace. The time is now to stop playing with the future of the human race. Each one of us must answer to God and to conscience. We must consecrate ourselves to God and God's peace, and if that means bearing the scorn of the realpolitikers, so be it.

For instance, it seems to me that when the Soviets shot down the Korean Airlines plane and, according to the usual customs of international diplomacy, precipitated a harsh re- sponse from the United States, the U.S. might have surprised the world by taking a new tack, speaking a new kind of language. What if the President of the United States had gone to Moscow to talk to the Soviet leadership to find out exactly what had happened and to make sure that they understood each other's positions instead of using the incident for propa- ganda advantage? We need, standing on the rock of the eternal, the Holy One, to speak a new language that arises from the divine depths of humanity's need to live, a language that speaks from the depths of the divine pathos. God does not want his vineyard destroyed. Listen to him elsewhere in the prophecy: "A pleasant vineyard, sing of it! I, the Lord, am its keeper; every moment I water it. Lest any one harm it, I guard it night and day; I have no wrath. Would that I had thorns and briers to battle! I would set out against them, I would burn them up together. Or let them lay hold of my protection, let them make peace with me, let them make peace with me" (27:2-5, RSV).

As I was exploring these ideas, quite away from any news sources, I was suddenly deeply moved by a vision of the divine pathos. It occurred, I subsequently discovered, at the same time as the bomb that killed 241 American servicemen went off in Beirut in 1983. I saw at the heart of history the crucified One, the innocent victim of our violence. I shuddered at the cruelty of history, "the slaughterbench on which are sacrificed the dreams of men and the honor of nations," as Hegel put it. Must it ever be so? Will only a remnant survive, resurrected from the rubble, wounded in hands and feet and head, limping in the twilight of civilization? We cannot know the future. The record of the past, however, is not encouraging. Perhaps God is again collecting his remnant now, and we shall not be spared the horror; we shall be doubly hurt, for we shall share the agony of God—rejected, ignored, heartbroken—the Holy One.

In the fourteenth year of King Hezekiah, Sennacherib, king of Assyria, comes up against all the fortified cities of Judah and takes them (36:1). Thus begins the end of Isaiah's prophecy. The overwhelming scourge has finally come. Rabshakeh, the Assyrian emissary, comes to Jerusalem and demands its surrender. Hezekiah, the king, comes to Isaiah the prophet. The prophet responds, "Thus says the Lord: Do not be afraid because of the words that you have heard, with which the servants of the king of Assyria have reviled me. Behold, I will put a spirit in him, so that he shall hear a rumor, and return to his own land; and I will make him fall by the sword in his own land" (37:5-7, RSV).

The army of Assyria is camped around Jerusalem. As far

as the eye can see, weapons and men of war, and the sun goes down on Jerusalem's despair. The sun goes down on King Hezekiah, on his knees in the temple. The sun goes down on this prophecy of Isaiah. And then the text continues: "And the angel of the Lord went forth, and slew a hundred and eighty-five thousand in the camp of the Assyrians; and when men arose early in the morning, behold, these were all dead bodies. Then Sennacherib king of Assyria departed, and went home and dwelt in Nineveh. And as he was worshiping in the house of Nisroch his god, Adrammelech and Sharezer, his sons, slew him with the sword, and escaped into the land of Ararat. And Esarhaddon his son reigned in his stead" (37:36-38, RSV).

God's power in history. It may be so with us too if, like Hezekiah, we return to God in quietness and trust, for "the Lord waits to be gracious to you; therefore he exalts himself to show mercy to you. For the Lord is a God of justice; blessed are all those who wait for him." Shall we be among those who wait for God?

CHAPTER SIX

THE BED IS TOO SHORT: ISAIAH

The bed is too short to stretch oneself on it, and the covering too narrow to wrap oneself in it.

—*Isaiah 28:20,* RSV

Struggle to get in through the narrow door; for I tell you that many will try to enter and not be able. . . . Yes, and some who are now last will be first, and some who are first will be last.

—*Luke 13:24, 30*

We are reminded by the quotations from scripture that we have not only to deal with the comfort of faith but also with its struggle and challenge. The ancient proverb that provides our chapter title shows that the prophet Isaiah, while uttering the direst warnings, is not without a sense of humor. He chooses an illustration from the most human level of our experience: the sleepless night on a bed too short with a blanket too small. Might as well get up and read. One turns over one way and one's back gets cold; one pulls the blanket over one's shoulders and one's feet freeze. Or one crouches all scrunched up in the fetal position and can't breathe. What an exquisite image of an impossible situation—and of course, as morning draws near and one hasn't yet fallen asleep, one becomes more and more desperate.

There is perhaps a more specific force to the proverb here than one at first realizes, however. It is not simply a general statement of an intolerable situation that no expedient can remedy, but also a specific warning of the coming of something that he calls "the overwhelming scourge": "As often as it passes through it will take you; for morning by morning it will pass through, by day and by night; and it will be sheer terror to understand the message. For the bed is too short to stretch oneself on it, and the covering too narrow to wrap oneself in it" (28:19-20, RSV). In other words, when the bogeyman comes, you won't be able to escape by going to bed and pulling the covers over your head, because your feet will stick out and he'll get you anyway. There is no hiding from this overwhelming scourge. His name is *Mot*, which means death, aka Assyria, that is, international power politics. Isaiah warns us that we cannot escape responsibility by refusing to think about the unpleasant things we seemingly cannot do anything about.

Isaiah is the prophet of war and peace. It is he who looks forward to the time when the nations "shall beat their swords into plowshares, and their spears into pruning hooks"; when "nation shall not lift up sword against nation, neither shall they learn war any more" (2:4, RSV). It is Isaiah who expects the coming of a son whose name shall be "Wonderful Counselor, . . . Prince of Peace," "when every boot of the tramping warrior in battle tumult and every garment rolled in blood will be burned as fuel for the fire" (9:6, 5, RSV). Isaiah is the prophet of war and peace, and although his hope for peace is timeless and his words have become vehicles for that hope down the millenia (Isaiah, I remind you, began his prophesying in 742 B.C., the year King Uzziah died), in his day he speaks to a very specific situation, and, like all of the prophets, does not mouth generalities. He believes that God has something to say about Judah's foreign policy in the latter half of the eighth century B.C., and he believes that he is to speak as God's representative and ambassador to the kings of Judah, Jotham, Ahaz, and Hezekiah, about their foreign policy. Isaiah believes that God has something of crucial importance to say in the matter of Judah entering into an alliance with Assyria for her own protection against the anti-Assyrian alliance of Israel, Damascus, and the Philistine cities of Ashkelon and Gaza, as Ahaz had done. It is this covenant with Assyria, this treaty, that he calls "a covenant with death." He believes that God has something important to say on the question that arises later during the rule of Hezekiah, Ahaz's successor, of whether Judah should enter into an alliance with Babylon and Egypt against Assyria, as Hezekiah eventually did.

The point is, the prophet always speaks to a concrete situation, and his message is moral and political. Therefore, those of us who are commissioned to expound these scriptures in the church cannot avoid political issues. Politics is too important to be left to the politicians. In a democracy, furthermore, it is the citizen's duty to be politically active, and as one of the institutions in our democracy, the church must do its civic duty. This need not mean that everyone in the church should be of like mind or that good people cannot differ honestly over important issues, but it does mean that we cannot pull the bedclothes over our heads and go back to sleep pretending that there is no problem or unwilling to face it.

The overwhelming scourge of our time is the same as it was in Isaiah's time twenty-eight hundred years ago: it is war. Therefore, statements like the pastoral letter of the National Conference of Catholic bishops, entitled *The Challenge of Peace: God's Promise and Our Response* and published in May 1983, and the pastoral letter of the United Methodist bishops, entitled *In Defense of Creation: The Nuclear Crisis and a Just Peace* and published in April 1986, are prophetic documents in the biblical sense. They speak God's word to our time. The Catholic document is aptly titled *The Challenge of Peace*, expressing the note of struggle that is inseparable from the attempt to be faithful to God's will and

53

purpose. God is challenging us in our time. We have an overwhelming scourge just over the horizon, much more terrible than the cruel Assyrians, unimaginable in its horror because it is unprecedented in all of human history. And it is we who have prepared it; it is we who labored to build it; it emerged from our own minds—our finest human intellects toiled together to bring it to birth, and now it waits with baleful patience for our permission to arise, to shine, and to shatter. It is the monster *Mot*, also known as death, also known as nuclear destruction.

I should explain this term *Mot*. It is the Hebrew word for death, and it is also the Ugaritic-Canaanite name for the god of sterility and hell. So when Isaiah accuses Ahab of boasting that he has made a covenant with death, there is the clear implication not only of unwise policy but also of idolatry. The implied message of Isaiah to Ahab is, "You have an existing covenant with Yahweh, our God, and now you have entered another covenant with the god of sterility and death, *Mot*, and you boast of this covenant, but it is a breach of faith; it is an act of treason against Yahweh. What's more, it's a stupid thing to do. You must have been drunk at the time." Isaiah says, "Addicted to wine, clamoring in their cups: priest and prophet are addicted to strong drink and bemused with wine; . . . hiccuping in drunken stupor; every table is covered with vomit, filth that leaves no clean spot. . . . It is all harsh cries and raucous shouts, 'A little more here, a little there!' " (28:7-8, 10).

Well, one might say, that is an exaggerated description of the foreign policy establishment—Foggy Bottom, the CIA, the Pentagon and the White House are not like that. Listen to what Isaiah says, and place it in the context of Washington politics: "Listen then to the word of the Lord, you arrogant men who rule this people in Jerusalem. You say, 'We have made a treaty with Death and signed a pact with Sheol [hell]; so that, when the raging flood sweeps by, it shall not touch us;

for we have taken refuge in lies and sheltered behind falsehood' " (28:14-15). The prophet assures us, however, "as often as it passes through it will take you . . . and it will be sheer terror. . . . For the bed is too short . . . and the covering too narrow." From this one you cannot hide. They actually boast in ancient Jerusalem that they had lied and tricked their way to peace. What a coup! Our problem is whether to join the anti-Assyrian alliance or not, they argue. What we'll do is, rather than oppose Assyria and rather than remain neutral, we shall make an alliance with Assyria. Terrific! A brilliant move! They make a treaty with the thing they fear most.

In Isaiah's time, the act of a covenant with death is, as we have just found, literal, rather than metaphorical as it is with us. Ahaz actually makes the treaty with Assyria when he is pressured to join the coalition of small states against Assyria. The net result of it is that he has to pay heavy tribute to Assyria and the net outcome is the Assyrian destruction of Judaea under Hezekiah. We have made a treaty with destruction in our time, metaphorically speaking. We have put our trust for peace and life in the monster of death and devastation. Isaiah's interpretation of God's will for his country is that Judah should stay out of all alliances altogether and trust in God. What, we ask then, is God's will for our time? Well, surely it is at least this: that we should not come to terms with death, that we should not make a treaty with *Mot*, that we should not put our trust for life in a monster of death.

I realize there is great danger in playing the prophet. Experienced people will tell us that political wisdom is really "a little more here and a little there." There is much truth in the claim that such bricolage is the way of the wise, not the staggering of drunkards, as Isaiah says; that indeed it is the prophets and zealots who start wars. So let us turn down the rhetoric and listen to God's word.

To the arrogant men who ruled Jerusalem, Isaiah says in

another extended metaphor, "Look, God is laying in Zion a block of granite, a precious cornerstone for a firm foundation, and on it will be carved the motto of this firmly founded edifice: 'He who has faith will not be in haste'" (28:16, AP). It is really a marvelous motto: "He who has faith will not be in haste," or, "He who has faith will not be upset, will not be shaken." Justice will be the plumb line and righteousness the plummet used in this building. It shall be true, therefore, in every sense. A society founded on faith, on trust in the living God, and structured by righteousness. In it people will be centered in themselves, on God, and related to each other with just the right blend of autonomy and intimacy. No one will tyrannize over another; the power of being will be properly shared. This will be a society of justice and compassion. So, Isaiah counsels, do not rush back and forth from *Mot* to *maweth* (Hebrew words for death), from death to lies, from Assyria to Egypt, from falsehood to fear, from nobody to nothingness. He who has faith will not be in haste, will not be upset, for "in returning [to God] and in rest you shall be saved; in quietness and in trust shall be your strength" (30:15, RSV).

I know, of course, that arms control is a complex matter, that peace is something to be struggled for and not magically produced by an incantation, no matter how profound. But this teaching of Isaiah about faith, about abiding in God, is not unrealistic. It tells of the foundation on which peace must be built: the foundation of personal peace. I believe that the most dangerous thing in the world is an unhappy person with power and that the second most dangerous thing is an unhappy person without power. (The latter are usually the victims of the former, the victims of injustice in society.) I don't need to remind anyone of that old ploy by which the unhappy transfer their personal insecurities and hatreds onto others, as individuals and as a nation. Thus, the United States makes the Soviet Union the focus of all evil in the modern world, both American evil—mostly American evil—and Soviet evil. Personal faith in God and justice in society is a realistic, if difficult to attain, basis for peace. If only such faith might provide us with leaders who are not unhappy in that deep, deep sense of off-balance, off-center, off-course, but who are centered, at peace, resting on the firm foundation that is faith in God; men and women who are not in haste, because they are in faith, and who do not rush from one delusion to the next, boast of covenants with death and hell, and take refuge in lies and falsehoods.

In Isaiah we have an example of faith applied to international politics. It is easy to scoff at the naïveté of such an approach. What difference does it make to Assyria that Judah trusts in God? The strong still take what they want and the weak, no matter how pious, do what they can and justice turns out to be, as an unnamed Athenian once said, the parity that exists only between those who are equally powerful. As Abraham Heschel writes in his chapter on Isaiah, "Faith is not an easy or convenient path. There are frustrations in store for him who expects God to succeed at every turn in history. But 'he who believes will not be in haste'—and listen to this— Enduring strength is not in the mighty rivers, but in 'the waters of Shiloah that flow gently,' (8:6)" (73). It is easy to scoff; faith is not an easy path. But consider this: Where is Assyria now? When last did you hear an Assyrian holy man from the eighth century B.C. expounded as if he had something to teach us after twenty-eight hundred years? Enduring strength is not in the mighty rivers—where is Assyria now? Enduring strength is in "the waters of Shiloah that flow gently" (8:6, RSV), because they flow quietly, deeply, tranquilly, irresistibly. Further, consider this: We are the Assyria of today, or the Egypt, if you like, the other great power of Isaiah's time. We are the mighty river. Where will we be twenty-eight hundred years from now, we who make covenants with the god of sterility and hell, who trust in death to give us life?

I have no simple prescription to provide. Let us rather listen to the prophet Isaiah and be moved by him to a deeper and more practical faith; let us hear his poetry and be inspired by it; hear the word of God as it came twenty-eight hundred years ago and as it comes today. What God is saying to us today is up to us to figure out together. No one of us is an Isaiah. But whatever it is that God has to say to us today, surely it has something to do with how utterly out-of-the-question is nuclear war; surely it has something to do with the urgent need for us to think and to feel differently deep down about the way we deal with our so-called enemies. The pastoral letters of the Catholic and United Methodist bishops, referred to earlier, are major contributions to finding out, as a Christian people together and as a nation of diverse religions, what the word of God is saying to us today.

We can, of course, make a start in our own lives. We can wait upon God in the faith and quiet trust of which the prophet speaks. We can let the gentle waters of Shiloah cleanse us and cool our ambition. We can take a stand for justice upon the cornerstone that is inscribed, "Whoever has faith will not be in haste," whoever has faith will not be upset, whoever has faith will not try in vain to pull the covers over their heads and pretend that the threat does not exist. He or she will, in the deepest place of the heart, accept as God's gift and God's task for life in this time, the challenge of peace.

CHAPTER SEVEN

THE DIVINE PERSON: JEREMIAH

Be patient with me and take me not away, see what reproaches I
endure for thy sake. I have to suffer those who despise thy words, but
thy word is joy and happiness to me, for thou hast named me thine, O
Lord, God of hosts.

—Jeremiah 15:15b-16

Hosea is the prophet of the divine pathos, Isaiah of the divine power, and Jeremiah is the prophet of the divine person, the divine presence. No one speaks to God as frankly and as freely as does Jeremiah, with the possible exception of Job, but even Job falls below the level of intimacy and humanity of these confessions of Jeremiah.

Among the material that makes up our Book of Jeremiah is a series of confessional passages in which the prophet speaks to God, unlike the other prophets who speak virtually always to the people on behalf of God. (The passages are: 11:18-23; 12:1-6; 15:10-21; 17:14-18; 18:18-23; 20:7-18.) These give us a rare glimpse into the prophetic soul. We overhear a man of God in private conversation with God, and what we over-hear is moving and deeply encouraging, for it tells us that even, or rather especially, the greatest souls suffer because of being caught in the middle of the controversy, the lover's quarrel going on between God and the world. In public Jeremiah takes the part of God against the world fearlessly; in private he confesses the strain and stress and complains of a burden too heavy for flesh and blood to bear. In public he is courageous, passionate, persuasive; in private he is frail, lonely, confused. He freely admits this, which is also an act of courage. Indeed, I think the courage of Jeremiah's public confession is rooted in the courage of his private candor. He knows himself, and he knows his God, and they speak together like two real people, real and believable; not mannered, not religious.

If there is only one thing we hear from Jeremiah, one lesson, one point, let it be this: God is real, a real person, the realest person we will ever know, and in his presence we should be, can be, real also. Hear how Jeremiah argues with and complains to God, accuses him, goes back and forth from agreement to disagreement. It is a lovers' quarrel, a good, honest wrestling of two people who can't live without each other but find it almost as hard to live with each other.

"Be patient with me," cries the prophet. That's only fair because, as he points out, "See what reproaches I bear for your sake" (15:15). Because of God, he is lonely. "I have never kept company with any gang of roisterers, or made merry with them; because I felt your hand upon me I have sat alone" (15:17). "Be patient with me, don't be angry. I've tried, you know I've tried," the prophet might as well be saying. "I have to suffer those who despise thy words, but thy word is joy and happiness to me, for thou hast named me thine, O Lord" (15:16). "Do you know what it is like to have the thing most precious to you despised, the source of your joy and happiness held in contempt?" he might have asked. "Do you know how that cuts at the roots of self-confidence, how it gnaws at the props of my life? Sometimes I wonder whether I am crazy. Why don't you take better care of me? Your hand is upon me; I sacrifice full participation in the human world for your sake. Why then is my pain unending, my wound desperate and incurable? You know what you are like? You're like a brook that's not to be trusted, whose waters fail—a man sets out across the desert trusting that when he needs water he will find the brook marked on his map, but he finds it dried up. You're like that, God, you're like that to me!"

God replies: "Will you stop this unreasonable complaining? Let's get back together. Then you will really be my spokesman; you shall stand in my presence and I will make you impregnable, a wall of bronze. I shall be with you to deliver and save you."

The prophet: "O Lord, my strength and my stronghold, my refuge in time of trouble, to thee shall the nations come from the ends of the earth" (16:19).

But Jeremiah later replies: "O Lord, you have deceived me, you have tricked me, and I have become a laughingstock. I thought you were going to defend me. So I will not think of you again nor speak for you, but no sooner do I say that than his word is imprisoned in my body again, like a fire blazing in my heart, and I am weary with holding it. I can endure no more. Easier to endure the scorn and derision than the fiery love of God shut up in my heart! O God, I can't live with you and I can't live without you. All my life will be controversy and loneliness, and I love you so" (20:7-13, AP).

Can we understand how profoundly true to life this divine-human relationship is? How important it is that our communication with God be true to life? If we do not speak the truth in our prayers—the truth about our anger and disappointment with God in addition to the truth about our joy and satisfaction, we show that we do not love him, do not trust him, think that he will go away and leave us if we tell him what we really think of him and who we really are.

I am not going to try to lay down rules of prayer or give instructions on the spiritual life based on this prophetic experience. The example of this vibrantly alive, utterly human relationship with God—human person to divine person—is sufficiently edifying. Look at it, let it sink in; let it seep into your soul. This is our God.

No one understood this prophetic relationship with God

better than did Martin Luther, the great reformer of the sixteenth century. He did not preach or lecture on Jeremiah. He lectured on Isaiah of Jerusalem and on the minor prophets, but not on Jeremiah or Ezekiel. Luther compared himself to Isaiah and his collaborator Philip Melanchthon to Jeremiah—but with reference to what he called his "temptations," Luther did see a parallel between himself and Jeremiah. He preached on Second Corinthians 3:4-6, the text of which, in part, is: "It is in full reliance upon God, through Christ, that we make such claims. There is no question of our being qualified in ourselves: we cannot claim anything as our own. The qualification we have comes from God." In this sermon, Luther referred to Jeremiah 20:14-18 and said:

> The office of preaching is an arduous office. . . . I have often said that, if I could come down with good conscience, I would rather be stretched upon a wheel or carry stones than preach one sermon. For anyone who is in this office will always be plagued; and therefore I have often said that the damned devil and not a good man should be a preacher. But we're stuck with it now. Our Lord God was a better man than we are. And so it was with Jeremiah [Jer. 20:14-18]. If I had known I would not have let myself be drawn into it with twenty-four horses. Ingratitude is our reward; and after that we still have to bother ourselves with the sectarians and give an account to God on the last day.

Robust, honest, larger than life Luther—of course he loved preaching, and he hated it. He preached in fear for his soul on the last day and in the joy of his soul kept safe in the grace of Christ, and he brought down a whole social order by his preaching. No wonder he was neurotic, constipated, devil-pursued, vulgar; conflict does that to a person. Beware the smooth preachers who love what they are doing, who do it with a smooth and steady self-possession. One may legitimately ask them which God it is they serve. But of the preachers of the Lord of Hosts, one may ask, "Show us your wounds"—for every servant of the true God is wounded, if not by nails and crown of thorns, then by other marks of the stress of God's controversy with the world and the world's rage against God or its icy indifference.

I thought it best to celebrate Luther, one of Christendom's great preachers, by using Jeremiah's prophetic experience, the archetype of the preacher's consciousness, to reveal my own understanding of what it is I do week after week, year after year. I know it is impertinent to include myself in that lineage, but that is just one more reason for the reluctance, the fear and trembling I feel at preaching—that by God's grace one should stand in a three-thousand-year tradition; that one should understand instinctively a Hebrew from the seventh century B.C. and a German from the sixteenth century A.D.— and think that what one is doing is the same thing as they were doing. The thought is awe-full and awe-inspiring.

Please know that when preachers speak hard things, dark things about human failure, human depravity, rage about our cruelty, chide and scold and say naught for your comfort, they would rather be doing anything else, anything else at all, because they do not wish to sit alone in controversy with fellow human beings. Preachers would rather do anything else than preach, but there is nothing else they would rather do. So, although in St. Paul's words, "there is no question of our being qualified in ourselves: we cannot claim anything as our own" (2 Cor. 3:5), preachers must preach; they are trapped between God and the world, a glorious agony.

Luther worried. Luther agonized at times: 'Bist du allein klug?' 'Are you the only one who understands?' he would ask himself. His last recorded words are:

Let nobody suppose that he has tasted the Holy Scriptures sufficiently unless he has ruled over the churches with the prophets for a hundred years. Therefore there is something wonderful, first, about John the Baptist; second, about Christ; third, about the apostles. "Lay not your hand on this divine Aeneid, but bow before it, adore its every trace" (Statius). We are beggars, that is true.

Beggars who must speak in God's name. May God have mercy on us, may Christ give us the words, may the Holy Spirit defend us—for your sake.

Luther knew that God is real, is a real person who feels compassion for his children and is involved in their agonies and struggles. He knew as Jeremiah knew, and as everyone who has the courage to take up the preacher's task knows, that there is a controversy going on between God and the world, and those who become involved in it must expect stress, rejection, anxiety, loneliness, and the deep satisfaction of being in touch with real people and the realist person of all, God himself.

CHAPTER EIGHT

WORDS LIKE A HAMMER: JEREMIAH

Do not my words scorch like fire? says the Lord. Are they not like a
hammer that splinters rock?
                                                    —*Jeremiah 23:29*

Do you suppose I came to establish peace on earth? No indeed, I
have come to bring division.
                                                    —*Luke 12:51*

These two sayings from the prophetic strand of biblical teaching are shocking and disturbing. From God we hope for words that heal, that soothe our troubled minds and build us up, words that unite us in harmonious families; but here are words that burn and break and divide.

Of course, the presence of these words in the Bible is essential to the credibility of its witnesses. Every mature person knows that life is a process of building up and breaking down and that the most valuable things we possess, especially the things that make up our deepest selves, often have to be won in struggle. The writer of the Letter to the Hebrews compares true life to a race: "We must throw off every encumbrance, every sin to which we cling, and run with resolution the race for which we are entered" (12:1). Strip down, leave all excess baggage by the trackside, and run! I remember some years ago seeing Mary Decker do just that, in a television report of her triumph in the three thousand meters at Helsinki, in August 1983. What a demonstration of discipline—that's what the Letter to the Hebrews calls it, *disci-pline*—the power of mind and body that masters pain, keeps on course, and reaches deep down inside to find that bit extra when everyone, including oneself, believes there is nothing left. Listen to these words from Hebrews 12: *resolution, endurance, opposition, not lose heart, struggle, resist, discipline, painful.* These are words that a world-class athlete understands very well, and perhaps also the many amateur runners who endure for the sake of satisfaction and a T-shirt. The unprecedented popularity of distance running in our time perhaps makes this image from the New Testament currently accessible to many.

The context of all three sayings we have quoted in this chapter is struggle: struggle against rival interpreters of the truth, struggle against persecutors and oppressors, struggle against loneliness and despair. I want to concentrate mostly on the Jeremiah passage, regarding the passages from the gospel and the epistle as corroboration of the centrality of this aspect of struggle in our experience with God. I want to concentrate on Jeremiah for two reasons: firstly, we know more about Jeremiah's situation than about the contexts of the other two sayings. And secondly, the phrase, "like a hammer that splinters the rock" reminds me of one of the great contenders against evil in our time, my friend Beyers Naudé of the Republic of South Africa. I shall return to him, but first the prophet Jeremiah.

In the book that bears his name, we have a collection of material from all periods of his life, some written or spoken by Jeremiah himself and some narratives about him, possibly written by his secretary, Baruch. Among this collection are six monologues in which Jeremiah bares his soul to God and to us, which were listed in the previous chapter. By analogy with a later work by Augustine, these six monologues have been called "The Confessions of Jeremiah." They are profound and moving. They tell in the first person of the joy of serving God and also, especially, of the terror and agony and loneliness.

Our Lord's words about the division within families that loyalty to him would cause could have been spoken by Jeremiah. In one of his confessions, Jeremiah hears the Lord say to him, "Your brothers and kinsmen . . . are traitors to you, they are in full cry after you; trust them not, for all the fine words they give you" (12:6). "You think I came to bring peace on earth? No, indeed, I came to bring division." In a heartbreaking outburst, Jeremiah echoes Job: "Alas, alas, my mother, that you ever gave me birth! a man doomed to strife, with the whole world against me. I have borrowed from no one, I have lent to no one, yet all men abuse me" (15:10). And here is a marvelously authentic cameo of faith and doubt, which we studied in the last chapter:

> I have to suffer those who despise thy words, but thy word is joy and happiness to me, for thou hast named me thine, O Lord, God of Hosts. I have never kept company with any gang of roisterers, or made merry with them; because I felt thy hand upon me I have sat alone; for thou hast filled me with indignation. Why then is my pain unending, my wound desperate and incurable? Thou art to me like a brook that is not to be trusted, whose waters fail.
>
> —15:16-18

We have at different times felt the joy of God's words in our hearts and also the loneliness and despair that brings us to the awful moment when we accuse God of letting us down, of being untrustworthy like a desert stream that fails to flow just when the thirsty traveler is most in need of water.

Words that scorch like fire and shatter like a hammer. Jeremiah had heard them in his own life with God. If he grew weary with contention and resolved not to speak in God's name again, he says, "then his word was imprisoned in my body, like a fire blazing in my heart" (20:9). And when he speaks the Lord is with him, "strong and ruthless." This strong and ruthless warrior has broken open Jeremiah's life.

No other person in the Bible is so open to us in his openness to God. And this is why Jeremiah begins his indictment of false prophecy in chapter 23 with the question, asked by God, "Can a man hide in any secret place and I not see him?" (23:24). False prophets are closed to God and closed to themselves. They admit no doubt. They are never heard to weep in anguish, to cry in desolation. They are never seen to tremble before God (while Jeremiah pleads with God, "Do not become a terror to me; thou art my only refuge on the day of disaster" 17:17). And the false prophets only prophesy good news.

Jeremiah lived in Jerusalem during one of its several periods of "last days." It had been sacked once by the Chaldeans and was under siege a second time for breaking the treaty imposed after its first defeat. The false prophets assured the king of his security, and they assured the generals of success at arms. Jeremiah prophesied defeat and advised surrender. The false prophets based their confidence on the traditional Zionist faith that God had pledged the throne of Jerusalem to David and his family and, therefore, would defend it against all enemies. Jeremiah had to stand not only against the irrationality of wartime propaganda and panic, but also against sacred tradition, against the fundamental, theo-ideological justification of his state. And he suffered the fate of all dissenters and defeatists in time of war.

But it is Jeremiah whom we celebrate twenty-five hundred years later as the revealer of God's nature and purpose, this defeatist traitor, Jeremiah, not his chauvinist counterparts; they are remembered only because of their association with him. And this fact alone should be to us a hammer blow that shatters our complacency. The Bible canonizes one who questioned not only the ordinary political wisdom of his time, but also the foundational theo-ideology of the state. History proved him right, but who could have known at the time? History proved him right, and his preaching provided the basis for a rethinking of the nature of God. The reason why God did not perish with Jerusalem and did not crumble with the throne of David is because Jeremiah, the prophet, had already detached the God idea from its identification with that city. And all that happened between 626 and 586 B.C.

In A.D. 1960, Beyers Naudé, the scion of an Afrikaner Nationalist family of impeccable political credentials, named for one of the extremist Boer generals of the second Anglo-Boer War, began openly to express his doubts about the theo-ideology of apartheid in South Africa. As a result of his study of the Bible and the influence of the ecumenical movement of the world church, Naudé could no longer square racial segregation with the gospel of Jesus. At that time, he was the senior minister of a powerful and fashionable congregation, moderator of the synod of his church, and a man marked for high political office in a party whose founder and first prime minister had been a minister of the Dutch Reformed Church. One of his sermons announcing this change of heart was on the text, "Are they not like a hammer that splinters rock?" And to his congregation he said, very humbly, very simply, "My friends, I have been broken, by the words of the Lord." Beyers Naudé the future minister of state became Beyers Naudé light to the nation, saint and martyr; for in due course, simply because of his political opinions, he was stripped of his office as a minister, expelled from his church, banned by his government. He has only recently been freed after seven years of house arrest.

His farewell sermon, preached in September 1963 to his powerful and fashionable congregation in Pretoria, was on the text from Acts 5:29. Peter and John answer the court that demands to know why they had disobeyed its order not to preach Jesus in Jerusalem. They say, "We must obey God rather than men." Beyers asks in his sermon:

But how does the person know that it is God who speaks? Through your conscience? And how do we know that our conscience is always right? How did Peter know this? How could he prove it? The fact is, he could not. He stands defenceless before his judges and before the people. All that he has as anchor is the inner assurance of faith which God has given him through his Spirit, and which he gives to all who after much agonizing are willing to stand in complete dependence before God, completely willing to be convinced by God concerning the obedience he expects from us . . . Time and again, at times with great agonizing, fear and resistance in my heart, the Lord brought me back to this part of scripture, as if he wanted to say, "Whatever this text may mean to others, this is my answer to you: Obey God rather than man" (1982, 100, 102).

And then Beyers Naudé descended from the pulpit and, before a stunned congregation, took off his robe of office and stripped away the symbols of his ordination. He found it necessary to do that, necessary to strip away the symbols of ordination in the Church of Christ in order to obey God.

There is a remarkable similarity between the experience of a Judaite priest turned prophet in 626 B.C. and an Afrikaner predikant turned prophet in A.D. 1963. Separated by twenty-five hundred years, they demonstrate how with God one thousand years is but as yesterday when it is past, or as a watch in the night. They show us that the mercy of God can wear a severe mask, that God is not indulgent but rather is challenging and exciting, demanding courage, resolution, and discipline.

The rocks that God shatters in our lives are always only the barriers in the way of our progress along the road of life, the inhibitors of our growing and changing, of our being transformed over and over again, each time nearer the image of Christ, the image of Christ crucified, the image of our true selves.

I cannot say precisely what the rocks are in an individual life that the word of God must shatter if that individual is to grow. Some of them will be burdens that must be laid down, opinions that must be allowed to change, goals that must be given up. At the extreme, like Beyers Naudé, one might have to allow God's hammer to shatter the assumptions that are the foundations and structuring force in life, and if that is the case, that person will know God as the terror, as the bringer of anguish. Some of the obstacles, on the other hand, might be absences in life, things needing to be taken up, friends to be allowed in, tasks to be done, study to be undertaken, space and time to be set aside for God.

Words like a hammer! God's words are always like that against our falsehood. So, paradoxically, it is a mercy, this hammer; it is a tool for making space, a tool for construction; and the division Jesus brings is a mercy that clears our minds and encourages our wills. At least we know at last that this way is a costly, strenuous way, a steep and narrow way, a way that is life itself. Therefore, "let us run with perseverance the race that is set before us, looking to Jesus the pioneer and perfecter of our faith, who for the joy that was set before him endured the cross, despising the shame, and is seated at the right hand of the throne of God" (Heb. 12:1-2, RSV).

CHAPTER NINE

THE DIVINE PROMISE: 2 ISAIAH

Listen to me, house of Jacob and all the remnant of the house of Israel, a load on me from your birth, carried by me from the womb; till you grow old I am He, and when white hairs come, I will carry you still; I have made you and I will bear the burden, I will carry you and bring you to safety.

—Isaiah 46:3-4

The collection of prophetic words grouped under the name of Isaiah contains material from at least three different periods: Isaiah of Jerusalem, who worked in the eighth century B.C., accounts for most of chapters 1 through 39, while Second Isaiah, who worked in the sixth century B.C. among the exiles in Babylon, is responsible for chapters 40 through 55. The remaining chapters are later still and are usually designated Third Isaiah.

All of the prophets we have considered so far have spoken in the face of a dire threat to the nation and have called people to repent in the hope that God would intervene and, because of their contrition, save them from disaster. For Amos, Hosea, and Isaiah of Jerusalem, this dire threat was bloodthirsty Assyria; for Jeremiah and Ezekiel it was brutal Babylon. Hosea revealed the divine pathos, Isaiah the divine power, and Jeremiah the divine person. Second Isaiah, whom we now take up, is the prophet of the divine promise, the herald of salvation. He wrote in the face not of a threat but of a promise: "We're going home, we're going home!"

"Comfort, comfort my people, [says the Lord]; . . . speak tenderly to Jerusalem and tell her this, that she has fulfilled her term of bondage, that her penalty is paid" (40:1-2). Thus begins his message. At last, you may say, we have a prophet who prophesies good news. It's about time! Here we have something to be thankful for, and so I would like to reflect on our festival of Thanksgiving in the United States in the light of this prophetic message.

We must be careful to give thanks for the proper things, careful not to make Thanksgiving an exercise in idolatry, in which we celebrate our country and congratulate ourselves. That happens when we are insufficiently aware of the true God, of the Lord of Hosts before whom we live and by whom we shall be judged. So it is a good thing for our souls that we put our Thanksgiving within a prophetic context in which we have heard the warnings of the prophets and have heeded, we hope, their advice: advice to be honest with ourselves, especially about our sins before God, and to repent; advice that self-righteousness is deadly and that the attitude that regards the opponent as totally wrong and ourselves as totally right is fatal; advice that was proven accurate by history—the disasters forecast by the prophets came to pass; advice that explains the root cause of disaster as the lack of faith in God. It is good for our souls that we place our Thanksgiving in the context of such honesty.

Such prophetic preaching is part of our heritage as a nation. No one understood this better than Abraham Lincoln, who proclaimed the first official Thanksgiving Day in 1863, shortly after delivering the Gettysburg Address; Abraham Lincoln, who in his Second Inaugural Address said in 1865, "It may seem strange that any men should dare to ask a just God's assistance in wringing their bread from the sweat of other men's faces; but let us judge not that we be not judged. The prayers of both could not be answered; that of neither has been answered fully. The Almighty has His own purposes."

No one understood better than Lincoln the treason of self-righteousness and its bane.

So the United States gives thanks, standing within the prophetic tradition and repenting of national arrogance, for the national good. Many in the United States are secure, prosperous, have much to be thankful for. Many are not enjoying good times internationally, however, and in my opinion our national arrogance is chiefly to blame. It seems that our present administration deliberately set out to create a situation of confrontation with the Soviet Union. Our rhetoric is fiercely self-righteous, scornful, haughty, contentious. We have called them barbarians, uncivilized, and evil. We have used tragedies like the downing of Korean Airlines flight 007 some years ago to promote not peace but war, as if the death of 269 people should be answered by yet more death. Recently I read with sadness an article in the *New York Times*, in which a British journalist, Jan Morris, who has loved and admired the United States since World War II—our courage and our generosity, our humility and our openness—tells of the awful moment when she could no longer deny what so many Europeans now believe, that the greatest threat to human survival is the United States of America.

So what shall we give thanks for? We shall give thanks for the prophetic word and for the divine promise. "You have been a load on me since you were born," says the Lord God. "I have carried you from the moment of your conception in the womb," says the Lord God. "Till you grow old I am He, and when white hairs come, I will carry you still; I have made you and I will bear the burden. I will carry you and bring you to safety" (46:4). What shall we give thanks for? We shall give thanks for that assurance. "I made you, therefore I take responsibility for you; and I will not abandon you before I have brought you to safety." Note the emphatic repetition of the *I*. In Hebrew it is even more telling than in translation, for the phrase *I am He* in the saying "till you grow old I am He" is the precise word that signals the presence of God in the cultus in the temple of Jerusalem, according to Leviticus. It is the technical term designating the divine epiphany, strongest sign of the divine presence, as well as being linguistically close to the divine name itself, the name of Yahweh.

Individually, we should find deep comfort in this divine promise. I have surely been a burden to God. He has had ample reason many times to put me down; I have been ungrateful, uncooperative, unpleasant, unwilling to hear. Many, many times he might have set me down and left me to make it on my own; but he created me, I am his child, and so he will not give me up. He will not wash his hands of me but will patiently bear the burden day after day, year after year, until gray hairs come and then the end; and he will still be there bearing me patiently, lovingly. What marvelous thoughts these are. So close to the heart of the prophetic understanding of God. God cares for the weak and the oppressed. God loves like a spouse and can be wounded by rejection. God is patient like a good parent and will not abdicate his responsibility for us. He made us; he is involved in our lives as individuals and as a nation. So what shall we give thanks for? We shall give thanks for this gospel. We shall give thanks for this revelation of the divine care, of the divine labor on our behalf.

As we give thanks for it, let us also put our trust in it, not only as individuals but as a nation, and not by becoming naive and irresponsible in our dealings with our adversaries, but by becoming sternly realistic. And what is stern realism? What is cold matter-of-fact reality? It is this: this God who bears us as a great burden will not give us up; this God can be trusted to honor any unself-righteous, honestly human attempt to live together with our fellow human beings. My objection to the present international policy of the United States and to preachers who support it on biblical grounds is that they pay insufficient heed to the Bible, especially to the prophetic word. They are lacking in faith; less than faithful, despite their desire to have prayers said in the public schools.

A few years ago when the aftermath of a nuclear exchange was portrayed on television under the title "The Day After," several religious and political leaders advised us not to watch it. Why do they not want us to know the worst that is possible? Because it will make us less than eager to support a policy that has "the day after" as the bottom line? Of course that's why. Those who plan such awfulness don't want anyone to know the extent of the destruction being planned. They do not even want to know it themselves. Why? Because dwelling on it would so appall us that we would lose our nerve and decisiveness? Because they believe that we have no alternative? I think both reasons are operative. But some of us believe that we do have an alternative: those of us who believe the promise of the Bible.

This is the same alternative that Isaiah of Jerusalem preached in the eighth century B.C., now being preached by another member of the Isaianic school two centuries later, in the sixth century B.C.: "Trust in God." (Ironically "In God We Trust" is emblazoned on our currency.) Our alternative is a realistic trust in God that affirms God's care for all the human race and affirms the humanity we share with the Soviets. Undergirding this common humanity and our solidarity with the Soviets in goodness and in sin is the God who bears us both on his back like two great burdens, like the idols Bel and Nebo of whom our prophet writes, who weigh so much that they make the oxen bow low to the ground, panting and sweating (46:1-2). God bows low beneath us both and bears us; he has not forsaken us, and if we repent we shall all live.

You think this is unrealistic? Think back several years to the moment when President Nixon, by one courageous act, transformed the People's Republic of China from a bitter and mysterious enemy into a friend. Think back to the policy of detente with the Soviet Union crafted by Nixon and Kissinger, and you will see what I mean. Progress in understanding and trust is possible. There is grace for living together: the God who bears us both, who bears us all. But the bitter-mouthed, ugly-hearted, faithless ones will never know it, and alas, they might destroy us all.

So the divine promise must be and is a promise for every contingency. Whatever awfulness we bring upon ourselves—and God knows the bitter-mouthed, ugly-hearted, faithless ones may yet have their way—God will bear us still, in life and in death, and that is the good news; that is the gospel of the God who bows so low that he can get under us and lift us and bear us up like an ox to its burden, low in a manger, low on a cross.

The difference between the true God, Yahweh, Lord of Sabaoth, and the many false gods, gods of sectarian nationalism and religious sectarianism, is well-expressed in the imagery of our prophetic passage. The false gods are a burden to us. We carry them around, heavy on our backs. We pay and we pay and we pay for them with blood and treasure and the substance of our souls, and they eat us up. They are a burden to us. But the true God, Yahweh Sabaoth, he carries us, and he feeds us and nourishes us and causes us to open and to blossom and to live and rejoice and to be strong, noble, beautiful. I recommend, therefore, as a test of faith, that you ask yourself whether the God you worship is a burden you bear or a support and a strength; whether the God you worship makes your heart heavy or makes it light; whether the God you worship towers over you like some threat or stoops to be with you like some friend. If he is the latter of these alternatives, he is Yahweh God of Hosts, the Father of Jesus our Lord. And if he is the other, it is an imposter.

Let God carry you. Trust, have faith, do not fear; and that does not mean to stop thinking and act naively, but rather to think and act and speak faithfully, not with bitter mouth and ugly heart, not with suspicion and distrust, but with faith. Think and act and speak faithfully, as if there were a God who has promised to bear us safely home, for there is such a God. He is our God. He has brought us this far, and he will not forsake us. "I have made you. I will bear the burden," says our God. To be mean and arrogant, to speak bitter accusations, especially these days in our international life, is to disbelieve in God.

For God has promised to bear us safely home, each one of us and all of us together. "Look to me and be saved, you peoples from all corners of the earth, for I am God, there is no other. By my life I have sworn, I have given a promise of victory, a promise that will not be broken, that to me every knee shall bend and by me every tongue shall swear" (45:22-23). The person who wrote this sees his people readying themselves to go home, to return home after seventy years of bitter exile. At last the hoped-for good day had come. Thank God, thank God!

And who makes it possible, humanly speaking? Cyrus, the unbelieving king of Persia, the Soviet Union of his day. "Thus says the Lord to Cyrus his anointed" (45:1). (The term for *anointed* in Hebrew is *messiah*.) To this unbelieving, godless superpower, the source of all their suffering, God says, "My messiah." "I will strengthen you though you have not known me" (45:5). The God who bears Israel also bears Cyrus of Persia, and even though Cyrus does not acknowledge God, God works his holy purpose through him. Thus are we all, believers and unbelievers, Americans, Russians, and Chinese, borne on the back of God, a joyous burden to him, all recipients of his life and his kindness. "Look to me and be saved, all you peoples from all corners of the earth."

Who are we, then, to set ourselves off in some bitter-mouthed, ugly-hearted, suspicious superiority? Because God has stooped to us as a parent to a child, as an ox beneath its load, in the cross of Jesus our Savior and in his cradle;

because God has stooped to us in Jesus, therefore every knee shall bow and every tongue confess Jesus is Lord (Phil. 2:11). Not because Jesus exalted himself, but because he humbled himself; not because he set himself above humanity in divine righteousness, but because in divine compassion and humility he identified himself with humanity. Can we do anything less? Therefore let us stop this arrogance.

This is the divine promise: "I have made you and I will bear responsibility for you, and I will not let you down." This is the divine promise. Let us give thanks for it. It is a promise not only for this life but for the life to come, not only for time but for eternity. This promise, this presence, Yahweh God of Hosts, this is our national treasure for which we give thanks, and it is not ours alone; it is the true treasure of all the human race. Thanks be to God.

CHAPTER TEN

THE RESOURCES OF THE SERVANT OF GOD: 2 ISAIAH

Here is my servant, whom I uphold, my chosen one in whom I delight, I have bestowed my spirit upon him, and he will make justice shine on the nations.

—Isaiah 42:1

The servant of God in Second Isaiah is one of the truly compelling figures of the Old Testament. His suffering, his perseverance, and his vindication by God have inspired countless believers. But who was he? Was there an actual man like this among those who were exiled in Babylon in the late sixth century B.C., when this prophecy was written? Or is he an ideal figure, a personification and a symbol of the people of God? Modern scholars have puzzled over the question of the servant's identity; the earliest Christians, however, knew exactly who he is: he is Jesus; Isaiah is prophesying Jesus; being a prophet, he is able to write about someone not yet born.

The servant figure is an ideal and a hope that was matched and fulfilled in Jesus Christ our Lord, and the early Christians show this conviction in the way they present the baptism of Jesus in the gospels (Matt. 3:13-17; Mark 1:9-11; Luke 3:21-22). Just as the Spirit is bestowed on the servant in Isaiah, so the Spirit comes upon Jesus, and a voice from heaven declares, "This is my beloved son, in whom I take pleasure" (Matt. 3:17, AP). In Isaiah 42:1 he is called, "my chosen one in whom I delight," and God says of him, "I have bestowed my spirit upon him."

Just as the prophetic tradition of ancient Israel influenced the way Jesus was identified, so did the tradition of the kingship. The declaration "You are my son" comes from Psalm 2, which is a hymn of praise to the king; in the course of this psalm, the king is identified as God's adopted son (vs. 7). So we have in the identification of Jesus at his baptism a combination of prophet and king, a recognition that he speaks with the authority of God and rules with the authority of the king. The image of the king impresses upon us the duty to obey his commands, while the image of the prophetic servant gives us a pattern of what that obedience might look like.

The gospels intend us to see in the life of Jesus a practical example of Christian living. To be sure, they do not intend us to do precisely the same mighty works that he did, but they do intend us to follow his example as it might apply to our own situation in the terms of the big images that Jesus represents. So when Paul says we are to die with Christ, he does not mean it literally, but he does mean it seriously. There is a spiritual attitude and a way of living that for us is a dying to self in imitation of his crucifixion. In the same way, when the gospels present Jesus as a servant, they are telling us that there is a service appropriate to our situation that Christ wants us to undertake; they also tell us that we can learn more about what it means to live as a servant of God by paying attention to the portrait that the prophet Isaiah painted of the ideal servant. Let us, therefore, take a long and careful look at the prophecy of Isaiah.

"Here is my servant; I uphold him; I delight in him; I give him my spirit." God's first word to his servant is a word of support, a list of the gifts that he gives to sustain his servant in the work that he must do. "God upholds me in adversity, in confrontation, in weakness, in loneliness, in fear; God upholds me. Underneath are the everlasting arms. God is pleased with me, and he gives me his spirit; God is with me." How often we forget this and fall into sinful anxiety! To be sure, such anxiety is understandable. No one who has sought to speak and live as a Christian in the sometime scornful and most-of-the-time indifferent intellectual community has not on occasion felt anxiety and despair. No one who has worked as a Christian in the so-called real world of commerce and industry is free of the tension caused by the dissonance between the gentle and selfless way of Christ and the merciless way of the world. For these good reasons, we should remember the first word of God to his servant: "I uphold him." However mild or acute our experience of this anxiety might be, to experience God himself upholding us, to be assured of his care for us makes us joyous in the midst of challenge, poised under pressure, and able to persevere.

I remember being in the office of the president of the college where I taught in the troublous late sixties, while crowds of chanting protesters threatened outside. The matters at issue were very complex; there was right on both sides and the president was under merciless pressure. He was a ruling elder in the Presbyterian church, and he confided to me then that the Calvinist teaching on the sovereignty and allsufficiency of God described what he was experiencing. He felt that God was upholding him, and I observed subsequently that he was able to maintain a gentle objectivity in the face of moral pressure, personal insult, and physical abuse. I saw him being spat upon. I remember Mark Curtis as a servant whom God upheld.

We all need to experience this divine support, but we shall not experience it unless and until we take up our calling to be God's servants. As soon as we undertake the risk of Christian witness and Christian service, we will begin to experience God's support. It is always tailored to the demands that are made upon us. Like the manna in the wilderness, it is suffi-cient for today's journey, and the greater the demand, the longer the journey, the more God upholds us.

I have noticed in counseling that I have done what I think is an instance of this tailoring of God's support to our need. Often Christians who suffer great blows seem to be composed and serene at the time of the greatest crisis, as if God's support were greatest at the time of the greatest need, as indeed I believe it is. Then, as time passes, the struggle to come to terms with the crisis gets personally tougher before it gets better, as if God were withdrawing his support as we become strong again, causing us to bear our own burden and finally to dispose of it responsibly ourselves. God's sustain-ing is always commensurate with our need, but it is never indulgent, never too much. "Here is my servant. I uphold him." Let us find a way to serve, and we shall feel the sustaining presence of God.

"Here is my servant. My chosen one in whom I delight." This is what a man says to his bride; this is what a bride says to her husband; to one's best friend: "my chosen one, in whom I delight. I have chosen you from all the people I have known. You are special to me, and I delight in you. You make me glad; you are joy and comfort to me; you are my friend, my beloved, my chosen one in whom I delight." A man to his bride, to his best friend. God to his servant. God to you and to me. God has chosen me; God delights in me. God has chosen you; God delights in you. He thinks you are special.

We are so good at convincing ourselves that there is noth-ing significant that we can do for God that we almost paralyze ourselves, so let us listen carefully to this prophecy and let it sink in: "I have chosen you, and I delight in you. You have a special place in my purpose, and I am very glad that you do." Can you begin to grasp this, to make it real in yourself? The divine delight in your being? The divine pleasure in your person? As the prophecy says later on in chapter 43, "I have called you by name and you are my own" (v. 1). When you begin to realize this, you will begin to know how important you are for God's work in the world.

Let me give you another example. An Oregon farmer with a heart condition, in his late fifties, went one evening with his wife and some of their children to a weeknight meeting at their Baptist church. There he heard of the awful plight of the mixed-race war orphans in the aftermath of the Korean war. He went home troubled; his wife went home troubled. They prayed, separately and secretly. As his wife said, they were careful not to influence each other. They sent money. They remained troubled. One night several months later, as they were going to bed, the farmer suddenly announced to his wife that he was taking money from their savings, that he was going to Korea to find children who needed a home, that he was going to adopt them and bring them back. "Funny thing," said his wife, "I was hoping you would say that; in fact I was about to suggest it myself."

Well, Harry Holt went to Korea and came back with seven orphans. The media recorded his arrival home, and the picture of him coming down the ramp with all those children in his arms caused such an outflow of compassion for those children and children like them that hundreds of offers of adoption were made to the Holts. Thus, the Holt International Children's Services of Eugene, Oregon, was founded—by a farmer who had a heart condition and was forbidden by his doctors to fly and by his wise and selfless wife, Bertha.

Now, more than thirty years later, after thousands of children have been saved and families enriched, Holt is bringing children for adoption from many countries and is also working hard for children in their countries of birth. The Holt Agency is supported financially and in other ways by many of us who now have a stake in Harry Holt's service. We are all empowered and enriched by his and Bertha's faithful servanthood. And he was just an Oregon farmer, chosen by God and delighted in as God's servant. This is surely an example of the importance of one or two individual Christians who will act out their servanthood in faith and with courage. The Holts were catalysts for a reaction of love and generosity. Their example tapped the reservoir of goodwill and lovingkindness that is in the heart of the church, in your heart and mine, in the hearts of us who want to serve in Christ's name.

Is there not something small or something great that has been on your mind to do? Do it now; you are God's beloved servant; he will uphold you in whatever you do for his sake. There is no satisfaction to compare with the satisfaction that comes from doing something for Christ's sake and seeing it have effects far beyond what you could have predicted or hoped for.

O God, since we know not what a day may bring forth but only that the hour for serving you is always present, may we wake to the instant claims of your holy will, not waiting for tomorrow, but yielding today. Consecrate with your presence the way our feet may go and the humblest work will shine and the roughest places be made plain. In the name of our Lord and Savior, your servant Jesus. Amen.

CHAPTER ELEVEN

THE TASK OF THE SERVANT OF GOD: 2 ISAIAH

Here is my servant, whom I uphold, my chosen one in whom I delight; I have bestowed my spirit upon him, and he will make justice shine on the nations.

—*Isaiah 42:1*

In the last chapter, we dealt with the first part of this verse, which tells us that God sustains his servants, delights in them, and chooses them for a special relationship with himself. We suggested that each one of us is a servant of God by virtue of being a member of the church, which is mystically the body of the perfect servant of God, Jesus our Lord, and so may expect the divine sustenance and affirmation that this text from the prophecy promises. The key that unlocks this resource is the willingness to act in God's service, the willingness to do and to dare for the cause of God. We saw an example of this in the work of Harry Holt, who was able to do great things for God when he took seriously the idea that he too, a simple Christian farmer not seemingly high in the ranks of the spiritual ones, was a chosen servant of God and could exercise compassion. Such is the servant's gift.

Now we take up the rest of the verse, which tells of the servant's task. Let us pay attention to the text. We are told, "I have bestowed my spirit upon him, and he will make justice shine on the nations." The declaration that the servant has the gift of God's spirit is a transition within this passage from the statements describing the gift—namely, that God upholds him, chooses him, delights in him—to the task, which is to bring justice to the nations. Listen to the servant's assignment. "He will make justice shine on the nations. He will not call out. He will not break a bruised reed. He will never falter. He will never break down. He will be a light to all peoples, a beacon to all nations. He will open the eyes of the blind. He will bring captives out of dark dungeons where they lie sightless" (vss. 1-4, 5-7, AP).

The gift: "I uphold him, I choose him, I delight in him." The task: "He will make justice shine on the nations." The link: "I have given him my spirit." That the servant of God has the spirit of God sums up all his resources and outlines all his tasks.

This assignment is so formidable that it is good to pause and take stock of the resources one more time, like the king going into battle or the man about to build a tower in the parables of Jesus (Luke 14:28-33). For, if one undertakes the work of God without the help of God's spirit, one is doomed to unhappiness and eventual failure. The tasks are so formidable, the difficulties are so great and require such patience and perseverance, such wisdom, that one cannot do them without invisible means of support. Please do not take this to imply that only Christians experience God's sustaining power or that only Christians do good works. All we are saying here is that those who make a difference, those who persevere in doing good are those who, one way or another, have made contact with the spirit of God and are sustained by him. We Christians do not have exclusive access to the spirit of justice, patience, perseverance, and compassion; but we do have real access, and we had better use it if we are to fulfill our duty as servants of God.

We believe that we have received the spirit of God and that that spirit assigns us the task—to bring justice to the nations. Notice firstly, then, that the horizon of our task is very broad. It is not my single self, my family, my group, my church, or my nation that is the horizon of my task as a bearer of God's spirit; it is the nations. From a Jewish point of view, the original point of view of this text, the horizon of our concern is the non-Jewish and even the anti-Jewish Gentiles. Here in a Jewish text sounds that note of trans-ethnic universalism that the Christian church made so much of in its early theology, as it sought to define its differences from ethnic-centered Judaism out of which it came. Justice is our task and justice's horizon is the nations.

The temptation to limit one's concern to a smaller horizon is very great, and for many reasons. One's native selfishness, one's sense that one has no power or influence over large groups, one's pride that will not endure the rebuffs and ingratitude that are part of serving strangers, one's sense of the futility of the task, of history as "the slaughterbench at which are sacrificed the ideals of individuals and the honor of nations," as Hegel put it. All of these, and other reasons we could think of, make the temptation to limit one's horizon to one's own concern very enticing. I may not be able to control the Soviets, but at least I can control myself. Or can I? Whatever the case may be, we Christians are forbidden to drop our eyes from the horizon. Such introspection may be allowed by some religions, but in Christianity it is forbidden, except as a brief retreat or as one part of a range of spiritual activities that includes a very large concern for others and for the nations.

Let me give you an example from my own life. I remember one summer evening long ago in the city of Chicago; I was sitting in my large third-floor study atop our attractive townhouse, surrounded by my books, with classical music playing in the background. I fell to musing on my good fortune; justice had indeed come to me within the horizon of my little world. Then through the open windows, wafted on a warm summer's breeze, came the sounds of Chicago's finest at work about a block away. Bang bang, screams, sirens, yells, sounds of running feet! The sounds of violence and death! Then I remembered that very early on in its history, the church had branded as heresy the attitude named gnosticism, which understood the work of Christ to be to save privileged individuals out of a world doomed to destruction. I remembered that my religion did not allow me to forget those out there embroiled in violence, shooting and being shot, killing and dying; did not allow me to forget that just like me they are beloved of God, people for whom Christ died, and that I could never be at rest as a Christian until all the world was just with the justice of God.

The gift of servanthood, that one is upheld by God and delighted in by God and filled with the significance of one's own being, entails the task. The Christian is essentially the servant of God's justice in all the world, and that means one is in a sense nailed to the world like Christ was nailed to his cross. The pain of the world must flow through us just as the joy of God and his creation flows through us. Perhaps it is in every one of us that darkness and light meet, that the redemption takes place; perhaps the line of meeting between the kingdom of God and the kingdom of the enemy passes through each one of us. We are essentially servants of God's justice in all the world because it is God's world; he made it, he loves it, he is present in it and to it, and he will not give up on it. We are not allowed to give up, either.

At this point I probably owe the reader some sort of definition of justice, which is a notoriously difficult thing to provide. We shall not go far wrong, however, if we begin our thinking about justice with a simple notion of fairness, even a child's notion, because children almost instinctively, certainly very vividly, grasp and express what it means to be unfair or to be the victim of unfairness, and they imply thereby that they have an instinctual notion of fairness. That notion of fairness, which one experiences perhaps most vividly when one experiences its opposite, is deeply implanted in human consciousness and is the locus of the meaning of the term *justice*. Although the idea has developed differently in various cultures and philosophies, what is common to all of these different expressions of the idea of justice is the sense that there is a right and a wrong way to apportion the goods of this world. This idea is closely linked to the sense that each human being has an intrinsic and inalienable self-worth, a common conviction that the apportionment should not be made in such a way as to violate the sense of self-worth of any participant.

Recently a Soviet dissident, Dr. Yarim-Agaev, raised the question, "Why did we, living in the Soviet Union, form the Helsinki Watch Committee to monitor human rights violations in the Soviet Union, knowing that we would never succeed in a system so skillful at suppressing human rights and human dignity?" He replied to himself, "We had to do it because nobody else would do it, and it simply had to be done." Well, why did it have to be done? It just had to be done. Something in the heart of humanity demanded that it be done—that something in the heart of humanity is the final locus of justice. The common conviction that all healthy human beings come to, that the apportionment of this world's goods should never be made in such a way as to violate the sense of self-worth of any participant in the world, that the dignity of the human individual is the absolute limit of the definition of justice, that any human organization that is worthy of the appellation *just* can never infringe on the sense of self-worth of the human individual. We are all precious in God's eyes; we are all beloved of God. Each one of us is one for whom Christ died; each one of us therefore is inviolate in our person, and however societies may be organized, justice demands that the maximum attention possible will be paid to the rights of this individual.

Our text expresses this somewhat indirectly, one might judge, when in verse 5 it seems suddenly to shift to the subject of the creation. Suddenly the text says, "Thus speaks the Lord who is God, he who created the skies and stretched them out"—you might ask, what do the skies have to do with justice? "Who fashioned the earth and all that grows in it"—you might ask, what does the earth and all that grows in it have to do with justice? "Who gave breath to its people, the breath of life to all who walk upon it"—you begin to understand what it has to do with justice. The shift from the servant and his justice to the creation only seems to be sudden; it is not really so. It is perfectly apt. We are reminded in it that the one who sends us out to do justice is the one who created us and all things and that in the Bible justice is ideally the state of creation apart from sin: the perfect harmony of man, God, animals, and plants that pertained in the Garden of Eden. Justice in the Bible describes the order of the creation as it came all new and fresh and shiny from the hands of God its maker. At the center of that creation stood man and woman in God's image, so any theory of justice, any practice that is just must honor the dignity of man and woman in God's image and must obey the structure of creation as far as we are given to know it through the veil of distortion, which is sin.

It is this demand that human dignity be honored that makes the dispensing of aid to the needy so tricky. It makes the element of justice in charity so difficult. St. Vincent de Paul, the great seventeenth-century saint known for his work among the poor in Paris, is reported on his deathbed to have said to the attending sisters, "We must be very humble and ask forgiveness of the poor, because we have given them charity." And we might ask about the justice of our charity, both public and private, in this light. Obviously, I have no formula to recommend that will, if applied, insure justice in our efforts as individuals, as a church, or as a society, to aid and to support those who are poor in our midst. No formula, but I can remind you, at least, of an attitude that should guide our thinking and acting in this regard, an attitude that arises out of the conviction that God our creator created each one of us with a dignity that is equal to the dignity of any other and is inviolate. Therefore, the poor have rights; they have God-given rights to the goods of the world. God's justice, you see, is not commensurate with human status. God's justice does not really care about human status within the structure of this world. It sees us all as dignified, with an absolute dignity residing or flowing from our creation and our redemption. And it is absolute in its bestowal of dignity on each one of us, whatever our status.

I am reminded of the history of the saints. Remember St. Francis of Assisi kissing the leper? Remember St. Martin of Tours giving his cloak to the beggar? Let me end with my favorite story from the Venerable Bede concerning St. Aidan and King Oswin of Northumbria in the seventh century, from Bede's history of the English church and people.

[King Oswin] had given Bishop Aidan [the Celtic bishop of Lindisfarne] a very fine horse. . . . Not long afterwards, when a poor man met the bishop and asked for alms, the bishop immediately dismounted and ordered the horse with all its royal trappings to be given to the beggar. . . . When this action came to the king's ears, he asked the bishop as they were going in to dine: "My lord bishop, why did you give away the royal horse which was necessary for your own use? Have we not many less valuable horses or other belongings which would have been good enough for beggars . . . ?" The bishop at once answered, "What are you saying, Your Majesty? Is this child of a mare more valuable to you than this child of God?" At this they went in to dinner, and the bishop sat down in his place; but the king . . . stood warming himself by the fire with his attendants. . . . The king turned over in his mind what the bishop had said; then suddenly unbuckling his sword and handing it to a servant, he impulsively knelt at the bishop's feet and begged his forgiveness, saying: "I will not refer to this matter again, nor will I enquire how much of our

93

bounty you give away to God's children." The bishop was deeply moved, and immediately stood up and raised him to his feet, assuring him of his high regard and begging him to sit down to his food without regrets. . . . The king sat down and began to be merry; but Aidan . . . grew so sad that he began to shed tears. His chaplain asked him in his own language [Irish] . . . , why he wept. Aidan replied: "I know that the king will not live very long; for I have never before seen a humble king" (1955, 164-5).

Justice is rooted in that absolute respect for the dignity of another individual expressed, I believe, so wonderfully in the question of Bishop Aidan—"Is this child of a mare more valuable to you than this child of God?"

CHAPTER TWELVE

THE STYLE OF THE SERVANT OF GOD:
2 ISAIAH

He will not break a bruised reed, or snuff out a smouldering wick; he will make justice shine on every race, never faltering, never breaking down, he will plant justice on earth, while coasts and islands wait for his teaching.

—Isaiah 42:3-4

We have seen something of the servant's resources and something of his mission, and now we shall consider his personal style as our text presents it to us. In a word, the style of God's servant is patience, humility and perseverance. He will not break a bruised reed or snuff out a smoldering wick. He will not falter or break down. Patience, perseverance, and gentle humility. So let us pay attention to the text, to its poetry and to its message.

The bruised reed. Slender and fragile at best. Someone has stomped on it. Its fibers are compacted in a bruise, and it can barely hold its head up, but it is not broken. The fibers are bruised, but they are intact; they can heal themselves, given time. That reed may yet live and bear fruit, unless some zealot for tidiness comes along and weeds out the weak so that the strong reeds may have space to show their style. The smoldering wick. It sputters and smokes and doesn't give much light, but it can be trimmed; it can be turned up and allowed to burn again more or less brightly. It need not be snuffed out and discarded.

We have two images from the house and garden of ancient Israel. Little things made littler by their exigency. Everyday things chosen to symbolize God's way with the world. A servant cherishes the little things, and that's how he brings justice to the world. These images carry a message that is important for us, I believe, with regard both to our activity in the world and with regard to our inner relationship with ourselves. Most of us believe—and rightly so, I think—that there is little we can do to contribute to the solution of the world's big problems. Nevertheless, the little things that we can do must be done. We must not break our little bruised reed or snuff out our small, sputtering light simply because they seem so weak and ineffectual. If our text is right, God's servant by God's Spirit makes these little things count for justice in all the world. We can at least try, ourselves, to be a part of the solution rather than a part of the problem.

Take the current concern about armaments, especially nuclear arms, as an example. People who are in a position to know have told me that the nuclear freeze campaign in which so many church and civic groups participated noticeably changed the attitude of the administration from one of more to one of less bellicosity. And many of the freeze's most prominent advocates knew that the freeze they were advocating was an unattainable goal. Nevertheless, it served to catalyze and focus human concern about the human future. A bruised reed, a smoldering wick, but a part of the solution rather than a part of the problem.

Let me say here that I think talk of solutions to great world problems is itself fraught with hazard. It may be that all we have and all we can hope for this side of the coming of the kingdom of God are bruised reeds and smoldering wicks. A few weeks ago, I was talking with a medical student who told me that he planned to specialize in psychiatry. I asked him whether he would not become discouraged in the long run, since mental illnesses are so notoriously difficult to cure and the success rate is so depressingly low. He told me in response that physicians spend most of their time treating the chronically ill, that medicine these days, instead of curing afflictions, principally enables the afflicted to cope with them. I believe that this is the case with most of the great scourges of the world. It is dangerous to believe otherwise, because such belief that the big problems can be completely solved usually leads to impatience, and impatience leads to rash action.

What, I ask, would a solution to the problem of nuclear arms look like? There is no solution. There is only the long, patient, careful struggle to cope, to manage. The problem, like a chronic illness, cannot be solved; it can only be managed. We cannot unlearn the knowledge that enables us to manufacture such weapons, and we can never insure that the weapons will not be used by someone at some time, but there are the lesser things that we can do, the bruised reeds and smoking wicks. We can try to prevent proliferation; we can be very careful not to upset the balance of deterrence; we can use restraint in every response, no matter how provocative; and we can do other vitally important little things. I think John Kennedy, in his great inaugural address, called our situation "the long twilight struggle." And in the twilight, my friends, even a dimly burning lamp is useful.

So much for the reference of our imagery to things in the world of politics, the outside world. What about their meaning in the subjective world of faith? The inward reference is just as telling. How often I come across people who are uneasy, sometimes even despairing, because they want to be Christians so badly but simply cannot believe everything they think a Christian must believe. Most of the people I know who have this problem are those who have tried the Protestant evangelical way of accepting Jesus as personal Savior and then have found their experience does not measure up to the wonderful new life they think they should have. Clearly, the fact that one cannot believe everything the faith teaches does not mean that one cannot believe something. Even though one cannot bring to God a sturdy stem of faith and a bright, shining belief, the Lord will receive the bruised reed that is the fragile yearning for God, and the smoking, sputtering vision of a better person. Be gentle with your faith, be gentle with yourself.

I came upon a recent book on Mozart by Wolfgang Hildesheimer. Hildesheimer, from a study of Mozart's letters, claims that Mozart died poor and depressed not because his poverty made him depressed but because his depression made him poor, that Mozart died convinced that his life had been a failure. What an astounding thought! We can all agree that the life of Wolfgang Amadeus Mozart was unequivocally not a failure. Yet, Hildesheimer writes, Mozart was so hard on himself, he lacked such gentleness with himself, that he came to believe his scintillating and wonderful gift had failed. I realize that this might be a controversial interpretation of the life of Mozart, but the example, I hope, stands. Be gentle with yourself. That bruised reed, that sputtering, smoking self, that yearning for God, that's the sort of thing that God uses to build his justice in the world if we bring it to him, offer it to him.

When the Lord told Peter to go out again to fish after a long night of fruitless toil (Luke 5:1-11), Peter was understandably reluctant, but it was just at this point of giving up that the catch was made. At the Lord's command, Peter took what he had and tried again. The servant of God perseveres with faith and with the cause of justice in the world. It is precisely this humble perseverance, despite our bruised and sputtering faith, that makes us part of the solution, part of the justice in the world, which we believe and hope will someday triumph, when in God's time God's kingdom is established.

So, my friends, let us bring to God what we have; let us bring to God what we can, of faith and of willingness to serve, of prayer and of work. Nothing we can bring will be rejected if it is the best that we can bring. The bruised reed he will not break. No, he will cause it to bear fruit. The smoldering wick he will not quench. No, he will use it and cause it to give light in that corner of the world where it is placed. As God's servants we, too, should cherish these little opportunities in the world and in ourselves, little opportunities for service, for faith and for adoration. We should make the bruised reeds bear and the smoldering wicks shine because they are all that we have, because they are all that we need. As God's servants, empowered and sustained by his spirit, we can make these little things serve justice in the world and be for us a satisfying and sustaining faith.

In conclusion, let me remind the reader that by doing all we can, we will be imitating God, which is what I think we are called to do by the statement that as God's servants we are gifted with God's spirit. Patience and perseverance are surely the essence of divine omnipotence. Because God is God, he can persevere and endure and outlast and outlove the strife of the world against himself. God's power is not coercive; God's power is conducive. It leads and attracts; it does not drive and threaten. It is essentially the gentle patience that does not break the bruised reed or snuff out the smoking wick. It is essentially the gentle attention that enables them to grow again and to shine anew. As God is, so is his servant. Therefore, let us be servants of God; let us accept God's sustenance and God's call, God's gift and God's task. Let us open ourselves to God's spirit and resolve to serve God's justice in the world, to work for fairness among people; and let us be very patient and very persevering and very gentle and very determined. Then we shall hear the Lord say of us too, "Here is my servant whom I uphold, my chosen one in whom my soul delights."

CHAPTER THIRTEEN

THE DIVINE PRESENCE: JOHN THE BAPTIST

[John the Baptizer says], "I myself did not know him; but he who sent me to baptize with water said to me, 'He on whom you see the Spirit descend and remain, this is he who baptizes with the Holy Spirit.' "
—John 1:33, RSV

In his commentary on Isaiah 11:2—the famous messianic text that runs, "The Spirit of the Lord shall rest upon him, the spirit of wisdom and understanding, a spirit of counsel and power, a spirit of knowledge and the fear of the Lord"—St. Jerome, the fourth- and fifth-century church father, quotes the apocryphal *Gospel according to the Hebrews* concerning our Lord's baptism as follows: "And when it came to pass when the Lord was come up out of the water, the whole fount of the Holy Spirit descended upon him and said to him, 'My son, in all the prophets I was waiting for thee, that thou shouldest come and I might rest in thee, for thou art my rest, thou art my first-begotten son that reignest forever.' "

The *Gospel according to the Hebrews* did not make it into the New Testament canon, probably because it suggested that Jesus was adopted as son of God at his baptism rather than born the son of God, as the emerging Christian orthodoxy believed. Nevertheless, I quote this apocryphal fragment because it attests to an important religious belief of Jesus' time, namely, that there was an identifiable chain of prophets down the ages, a chain of prophets that culminated in Jesus. In

Jesus' time, people viewed the prophets as revealers of God. The Christians saw Jesus as belonging to that revelatory tradition not just as one more prophet in the series, but as the culmination and climax of it. In him, the whole fount of the Holy Spirit came to rest and to dwell. In the other prophets, something less than the whole fount merely visited from time to time, rather than dwelt.

We have seen that each prophet emphasized a part, one aspect, of the divine nature: the divine justice, the divine compassion, the divine power, the divine promise. But now we approach the mystery itself, the divine presence in his fullness. Or rather, he approaches us. The promise is about to be fulfilled. Our verb tenses are about to shift from future to present. And at the point of entry to the promised land of the divine presence stands the last of the old prophets and the first of the new: John the Baptizer.

His place of work down by the Jordan fords is almost literally where Joshua and the people of Israel crossed the river when they first entered the Promised Land one thousand years before. His place of work by the Jordan fords is also precisely where Elijah, the first of the prophets, had, according to tradition, been taken up to heaven in a chariot of fire (2 Kings 2:11). John is, therefore, the man of the new beginning standing at the place of new beginnings—the place of Joshua. He is also the man of endings standing at the place of ending, where Elijah was taken up to heaven in a chariot of fire.

It is interesting to note that the Roman god of gateways and doors, named Janus, has two faces, one looking backwards and one looking forwards, one to the past and one to the future. The New Testament cannot make up its mind whether John belongs to the old dispensation or the new, whether he is Elijah or not. Matthew 11:13-14 says he is Elijah; John 1:21 says he is not; that the New Testament cannot make up its mind seems to me to suggest that the truth that Janus symbolizes pertains to the New Testament in this case.

John, like every gatekeeper, has two faces: he stands at the end and he stands at the beginning. He stands at the end of the journey and at the beginning of the celebration. One has journeyed long to come at last to the door. As one enters the door, one begins the event, the celebration. So doorways and gateways are places of endings and beginnings, and the doorkeepers look backward and forward. John the Baptist is Elijah standing now as Elijah once stood at the inception of the series of prophetic revelations, standing now at the threshold of the revelation of the very divine presence himself. But he is not Elijah, because he is the end of the old order. "Truly, I say to you, among those born of women there has risen no one greater than John the Baptist; yet he who is least in the kingdom of heaven is greater than he" (Matt. 11:11, RSV). What a poignant saying! John is the end, he is the beginning. As Moses stood on Mount Pisgah and saw the Promised Land but didn't enter it, so John, the preparer of the way, was humbly doing what I suppose today would be called "advance man work" for the real candidate.

Now I hope that we who stand near the end of our reflections on the chain of the prophets might also be standing at the beginning of a new understanding of God, might experience a beginning and an end, an end and a beginning. I hope that hearing the prophetic witness that God is full of divine compassion for humanity, that God needs and wants human sympathy and love in return might be for us an end of ideas of God that have not really worked for us, ideas of an exalted God uninvolved in human life, uncaring about human response, a punishing father; ideas of God that have made belief more difficult rather than easier. May there be for us an end to old and no-longer-useful ideas about God, a smashing of the idols. That would be a good prophetic thing to do. And may there be the beginning of a new idea, a new experience, and a new freedom as we enter into the loving humility of God in our midst, the surprising otherness of the closeness of God in our ordinary lives.

May our hearing of the prophetic witness be an end and a beginning as it causes us to realize that no matter how painful and unpeaceful it may be, God does take sides in politics and we must do so too; that we cannot love everyone in an un-principled conflict-avoiding way; that the divine compassion participates in history often in a partisan way, at least taking the part of the victims against the victimizers.

May our hearing of the prophetic witness have brought us an end and a beginning in bringing us to repentance, to that deep, deep change of mind in which, with God's help, we shift our focus of attention from self to God; a deep change of mind by which God becomes our all-sufficient joy. Repen-tance as end and beginning, as change of heart and of mind.

Abraham Heschel, who has been my guide through many of these meditations, sums up "the divine pathos" as follows:

> Pathos means: God is never neutral, never beyond good and evil. He is always partial to justice. . . . It is something the prophets meet with, something eventful, current, present in history as well as in nature. . . . In sum, the divine pathos is the unity of the eternal and the temporal, of meaning and mystery, of the metaphysical and the historical. It is the real basis of the relation between God and man, of the correlation of Creator and creature, of the dialogue between the Holy One of Israel and His people (231).

Where shall this pathos of God be found? Eventful, cur-rent, present in history as well as in nature? John the Baptist answers for all prophets when he tells the authorities sent to question him, "It is not I. I am not the one." John proclaims the end of the prophetic tradition.

John's denial expresses the humility of the prophetic word,

the fact that the prophetic word knows itself to be merely word and not the reality to which word points, merely promise and not fulfillment, always pointing beyond itself to the one who is to come, to the promised one. And who is this promised one in which the divine pathos is encountered as the divine presence? Who is this one in whom divine pathos becomes divine presence? Pointing to Jesus, John answers, "Behold, the Lamb of God, who takes away the sin of the world" (John 1:29, RSV). And if, as Heschel writes, the divine pathos is the unity of the eternal and the temporal, of meaning and mystery, of the metaphysical and the historical, then we Christians, helped by these words of a Jewish theologian, point with John to the Savior Jesus as the locus of the divine pathos, the one in whom for us the passionate love of God is there, as event and as presence; and we say, "Behold!"

The prophets saw the divine pathos in the suffering of the oppressed and the unhappiness of the family, in war and in politics, in the human things of human life, but most especially in suffering love that is the necessary mode of the divine presence to a rejecting world. Karl Barth, the famous Protestant theologian, worked always with a representation of the Isenheim altar at Colmar in Alsace, France, near at hand. It is a representation by Mathias Grünewald which portrays a grotesquely suffering Christ in the mode of the late German middle ages and John the Baptist with an enormous index finger pointing to the cross while a lamb stands at his side. There, John is showing, God revealed his presence in the heart of human history as suffering love that bears and bears away the sins of the world. Behold the Lamb of God!

If one pays close attention to the prophetic word that we have been studying in these chapters, one will realize that virtually all of the prophets went unheeded. The disasters they warned against came to pass. Even the promise of God that they delivered was for the most part ignored, misused, and taken for granted in its very coming to pass. All of the prophets were, from a worldly point of view, failures. And finally, as a culmination of this labor of self-giving and self-revealing, God comes himself, no longer to warn and to plead in word and symbolic action, because he knew that his warnings and his pleadings were making no real difference. Now God comes to take upon himself and to transform from within our hostility against each other, our hatred of life, and our rage against himself. If human beings will not be spoken to, God says, then they must be spoken with, for I will not give up on them and I will not give them up.

So John points us to God's saving action on the cross, an event that reveals our hostility to life and our hatred of God. John points us away from the surface structures that our deceitful power has raised, away from wars and governments and high finance, to a baby in a manger and a young man outside the city on a cross. He points beneath the surface of power and prestige to the place where we are all human together, or where we all can be human together, to a birth and to a death, to the time when we are all naked and in need of one another, the time of our birth and death.

It is impossible to unpack the whole meaning of the fulfillment that Christian faith sees in Jesus. Nevertheless, we can say that John the Baptist's pointing finger points on behalf of Amos and Hosea, on behalf of the Isaiahs and Jeremiah, Ezekiel and Elijah. "Behold the Lamb of God that bears away the sin of the world!" Behold the God whose pathos and compassion, whose love for us and desire for our happiness brings him into the most intimate union with us! Behold the word, the prophetic word, made flesh! As the letter to the Hebrews puts it, "In many and various ways God spoke of old to our fathers [and mothers] by the prophets; but in these last days he has spoken to us by a Son, whom he appointed the heir of all things, through whom also he created the world" (Heb. 1:1-2, RSV). He has spoken to us by a son. "Behold the Lamb of God!"

A word of gentle presence, a word made flesh, a power more profound than all the powers of the world to renew, to transform you and me. And so let us turn with John, the preparer of the way, to the God of the prophets as he draws near, very near, to you and to me. Let us turn in preparation and in prayer, that the presence of the God of the prophets now made flesh in Jesus our Savior may heal and sustain and save us. Jesus Christ, Lamb of God, divine presence; "My Son in all the prophets, I was waiting for thee, that thou shouldest come, that I might rest in thee, for thou art my rest." May we, too, be able to say that; in all the prophets we have been waiting for you, Lord Jesus. You are our rest. Let us enter in.

CHAPTER FOURTEEN

THE OFFENSE OF JESUS

"Who is this?" people asked, and the crowd replied, "This is the prophet Jesus, from Nazareth in Galilee."
—Matthew 21:10-11

Our Lord began his last week on earth by riding into the holy city on a donkey and overturning the tables of the money changers and animal vendors in the temple. For Christians this is the most significant week in the history of the world. By Thursday Jesus would be having his last supper with his disciples, and by Friday he would be dead; the next week, on Sunday, the world began again, the new world of life and immortality, the world of Easter.

One of the more intriguing questions is, "Why did they kill Jesus? What was his offense?" There was certainly a dramatic change in the crowd's attitude to Jesus between Palm Sunday and Good Friday. One day they hailed him as a celebrity, the other day they called for his execution without hesitation or apparent remorse. What was the offense that caused that swing of mood on the part of the crowd?

This is more than merely an historian's question; it is a question that our faith asks, as well as our minds. What do we find so offensive in Jesus that we wish to kill him in order to be rid of his challenge? This is the way faith frames the question, for in the realm of faith, all is simultaneous. We today are part of the crowd that found him so intolerable then; we are one with those who crucified him; those ancient

Jerusalemites are our representatives and surrogates. What is the offense of Jesus?

Perhaps some reflection on the past, on the events of that first Holy Week will help us to find an answer to our present question. What offense do they find in Jesus then? What offense so severe that they turn him over to the authorities to be executed? Is it the contravention of some law? Is it a political threat to the powers that be? Why do people hail him one day and reject him five days later? Let us look at the evidence.

As pilgrims approach the holy city, Jerusalem, coming in awe and rejoicing to the head of the steep road up from Jericho, they always dismount from their conveyance and enter the holy city on foot. There are rabbinic laws from the period exempting the infirm from the duty of pilgrimage to Jerusalem because they could not be expected to walk the last part of the way. From this fact we learn that it was more than a custom, it was almost a law, and certainly an act of piety, to dismount and enter the city on foot. In 1898, Kaiser Wilhelm II of Germany deeply affronted the feelings of the inhabitants of Jerusalem when he rode into the city on a splendid white horse. (His effrontery knew some bounds, however; at least he did not ride in on an ass.) In contrast, the British General Allenby, who accepted the surrender of the city from the Turks in 1917, dismounted when he came close and made the final entry on foot.

By now the point is obvious; Jesus, rather than dismounting to enter the city on foot, walks up to the boundary of Jerusalem and carefully and deliberately mounts up and rides into the city. He does the very opposite of what respect would require; and the fact that he rides on a donkey does not make it a humble event, for donkeys were accepted conveyances for Israelite royalty. Furthermore, he comandeers the donkey— "Our master needs it" is what the disciples are to say to the owner of the donkey if he challenges their right to take it—

and the right to comandeer is the right of the king under Israelite law. The evangelist sees this act as a deliberate fulfillment of the prophecy in Zechariah 9:9, "Tell the daughter of Zion, 'Here is your king, who comes to you in gentleness, riding on an ass, riding on the foal of a beast of burden' " (Matt. 21:5). This is what the evangelist Matthew makes of the scene. What do you think the average observer would have made of it? I think the observer would see it as an extraordinary display of personal authority, probably as an intolerable act of self-assertion, of disrespect for the conventions and proprieties governing the behavior of pilgrims, a disregard of the sensibilities of decent people. One would know that it is being done deliberately and not carelessly; this is not the act of an ignorant slob who is simply too uncouth to know or care what decent behavior demanded. This is the intentional act of a thoughtful man who by these means is making a statement. It is that statement that caused the fatal offense. What is it?

Let us follow Jesus to the end of his ride. He does dismount eventually, at the temple; and there he leaps off in apparent anger and attacks the money changers and vendors of sacrificial animals, overturning their tables and driving them out of their places of business. Now, since there are scores of such businesses in operation at any one time, and since we are told that Jesus acted alone and without a plan of assault, this act is symbolic rather than practical. Only one or two businesses are disrupted by the onslaught. Jesus is not cleansing the temple as most of our thoughtless commentaries assure us; he is rather making a statement by means of a public symbolic act. What is that statement?

We have no reason to believe that these money changers and animal vendors are crooks, and we know that they are not merely souvenir sellers like those who desecrate so many of the sacred sites of our civilization today. Rather, they are an integral and essential part of the system of sacrifice that is the

111

temple's reason for being. They change the currency of the pilgrims from all over the world into the standard currency of the temple so that they can purchase sacrificial animals from vendors who offer animals that are guaranteed to be unblemished and therefore acceptable for sacrifice. This is a great convenience; indeed, it makes the whole process of the offering of sacrifice possible for pilgrims who cannot realistically travel with sacrificial animals and risk that they would be declared unfit after all the effort of the journey.

An attack upon the people who provide this service, therefore, is not merely an attack on the abuses of the temple, but rather, it is an attack upon the temple's very reason for being, an attack upon the sacrificial system itself. Jesus proclaims by means of a public symbolic act that he has come to bring the sacrificial system to an end and to destroy the temple. "'Who is this?' people asked, and the crowd replied, 'This is the prophet Jesus, from Nazareth in Galilee.'"

These observers remember that the technique of public symbolic acts was a characteristic method of the great prophets of old. They remember that Hosea had married a whore to show how God loved his unfaithful people; that Isaiah had gone about naked and barefoot for three years to symbolize what the king of Assyria would do to the king of Egypt and so to discourage Judah from entering into an alliance with Egypt (Isa. 20:1-6); that Jeremiah wore a yoke of wood around his neck to dramatize the fact that the king of Judah would soon be under the yoke of the king of Babylon (Jer. 27:1-3); and that Ezekiel did not grieve for his wife when she died to show that God would not grieve over the coming destruction of the temple (Ezek. 24:22-24). Jesus the prophet from Nazareth in Galilee comandeers an ass, rides into the holy city and makes a token attack on the sacrificial system to proclaim its overthrow. He acts like a prophet, and his message costs him his life.

Now at last we know what the offense of Jesus is. Speaking

with the authority of a prophet, he declares that God is through with the existing religion of sacrifice and will soon destroy the temple. That prophecy is fulfilled within forty years as the temple is destroyed, and to this day the temple has not been rebuilt. In his trial, Jesus is accused of threatening to destroy the temple himself, obviously a garbled version of the general threat against the temple that he made. This alone would be reason for the guardians of temple religion to have him killed, but what would cause the Romans to collaborate in his murder? That cause is given by Jesus' riding into the city on a comandeered ass, an action that claimed a kingly dignity. That is why Pilate's chief question to Jesus is, "Are you a king?" and why the title on the cross is "King of the Jews."

Enough history for the moment. I hope that readers have found it helpful to understand these events as the events might have happened and as they might have been understood in those days. For our day, the offense of Jesus is essentially the same as it is then. He speaks to us as prophet with the authority of God; he does away with the sacrificial attitude in our lives, the attitude that is always transferring responsibility for our own sins onto somebody else and reveling in revenge and victimization; and he rules our wills and destinies as a mighty king. Jesus, our prophet, our priest, and our king, demands of us absolute loyalty to his person, and this is the offense of Jesus.

We find it odd and unacceptable that the truth of God should be focused so narrowly on one figure, that all the powers of the universe should concentrate and be available to simple trust in this one person; that the profoundest and most fulfilling human act should be plain loyalty and passionate commitment to this one man. But that is the Christian secret, the claim and the truth of the gospel. In this Jesus, "the complete being of God, by God's own choice, came to dwell. Through him God chose to reconcile the whole universe to

113

himself, making peace through the shedding of his blood upon the cross—to reconcile all things, whether on earth or in heaven, through him alone" (Col. 1:19-20). Jesus is for us the word of prophecy, the comfort of priesthood and cultus, and the authority of the kingship. He is everything to us in life and in death. He is our Lord and our God. This is his offense and it is our fulfillment. For us who are not offended but ready in faith to accept his claim, Jesus is indeed all that he claims to be. This is the clear claim and offer of the gospel; this is the power of our religion. And so let us grasp it anew and experience anew the power of life that is in this man Jesus.

Alice Meynell ends her great poem "Christ in the Universe" this way: she imagines a day when all sentient beings from all the galaxies come together to compare their experiences of God. She writes:

> But, in the eternities,
> Doubtless we shall compare together, hear
> A million alien Gospels, in what guise
> He trod the Pleiades, the Lyre, the Bear.
>
> Oh be prepared my soul!
> To read the inconceivable, to scan
> The million forms of God those stars unroll
> When, in our turn, we show to them a Man.

WORKS CITED

Bede. *A History of the English Church and People*. Translated by Leo Sherley-Price. Revised by R. E. Latham. London: Penguin Books, 1955.

Heschel, Abraham Joshua. *The Prophets* New York: Harper & Row, Publishers, 1962.

Randall, Peter, Editor. *Not Without Honor, Tribute to Beyers Naudé*. Johannesburg: Ravan Press, 1982.

Terrien, Samuel. *The Elusive Presence: Toward a New Biblical Theology*. New York: Harper & Row, Publishers, 1978.

ABOUT THE AUTHOR

Dr. Robert Hamerton-Kelly is Senior Research Associate at the Center for International Security and Arms Control of Stanford University. He is an ordained minister in the United Methodist Church and has previously held the positions of Dean of Chapel at Stanford University, professor at McCormick Seminary in Chicago, and assistant professor at Scripps College in Claremont, California.

Dr. Hamerton-Kelly has received an undergraduate and a master's degree from Cambridge University and a doctoral degree from Union Theological Seminary in New York. He is also the author of *Sprung Time* for The Upper Room, *God the Father: Theology and Patriarchy in the Teaching of Jesus*, and *Pre-existence, Wisdom and the Son of Man*.